LIVING READY
POCKET MANUAL

FIRST AID

FUNDAMENTALS
FOR SURVIVAL

), M.D., M.P.H.,
. DOCTOR™

BOOKS
ONSIN
www.LivingReadyOnline.com

IMPORTANT DISCLAIMER

Please read before using this book.
Use of the information in this book is *at your own risk*, intended solely for self-help, in times of emergency or when medical help is not available, and does not create a doctor-patient relationship.

 Do not use this information instead of seeking the help of qualified medical personnel.

Readers are strongly cautioned to consult with a physician before acting on the information described in this book. This book is based on information from sources believed to be reliable, and every effort has been made to make the book as complete and as accurate as possible based on information available as of the publication date, but its accuracy and completeness cannot be guaranteed. Despite the best efforts of the author and publisher, the book may contain mistakes, and the reader should use the book only as a general guide and not as the ultimate source of information about the subject of the book.

The book is not intended to reprint all of the information available to the author or publisher on the subject, but rather to simplify, complement and supplement other available sources. The reader is encouraged to read all available material and to learn as much as possible about the subject.

The author and publisher are not engaged in rendering medical services, and the book is not intended to diagnose or treat medical or physical problems. If medical, professional or other expert assistance is required by the reader, please seek the services of a competent expert.

This book is sold without warranties of any kind, express or implied, and the publisher and author disclaim any liability, loss or damage caused by the contents of this book.

CONTENTS

6. REACTIONS: ANAPHYLAXIS, SKIN IRRITATIONS AND POISONING 130

INTRODUCTION

You're starting a campfire. Suddenly there's an explosion and your pant leg is on fire—the searing pain and the burning flesh is yours. What do you do? In situations like this, even the best of us usually panic, if only for a few seconds. We might run or try to pat out the fire with our hands. Who knows? For a fraction of time we stop thinking rationally, and those around us do, too. Fortunately, someone in the group typically gathers his senses quickly and smothers the fire with water or a blanket or a roll on the ground.

REACTING TO MEDICAL EMERGENCIES

The way I see it, there are two problems with medical emergencies.

1. You never know when they're coming.

2. You don't know what kind of health threat they will cause.

You could be firing up your grill, chopping vegetables in your kitchen or going on the same hike you've been on ten times before when BAM, out of nowhere, the grill explodes, you drop the knife and cut your foot, or you fall and hurt your ankle. We don't expect everyday activities to turn into emergencies, but they often do.

And you could train to know everything there is to know about treating a broken bone or a head injury and then have an allergic reaction to a bee sting or cut an artery in your leg.

Emergency situations are unplanned and unpredictable, which can cause you to panic even if it's only for a few seconds. Your body goes into fight-or-flight mode. It's one of our most basic survival skills. Adrenaline kicks in, your heart speeds up, your muscles tense. And all that extra blood flow and energy goes into your muscles and leaves your brain, slowing your mental reaction, if only for a moment.

PREPARING FOR MEDICAL EMERGENCIES

So, how do you prepare for the unexpected? What can you do to regain your focus and make smart, lifesaving decisions as quickly as possible in an emergency? I propose you prepare in the same way medical doctors prepare, by following these two steps.

1. Memorize the basics of first aid.

There are a few basic first aid procedures and principles doctors memorize early in their training. The point is to make these lifesaving skills their natural reaction to a medical emergency.

Memorize steps for how to handle a few common problems—learn how to administer CPR, how to help someone who's choking and how to treat a cut, a burn and a broken bone. Much of this information is covered in this little book, and I've highlighted the important steps you need to memorize. Don't worry, each step is not more than a line or two.

Following these basic procedures will buy you time in an emergency and help improve the odds of survival if you face a medical emergency. Many of the basic treatments for the most common injuries are not that difficult to perform, and you can learn to do them very well. Knowing one or two basic treatments and performing them in an emergency can change an injured person's status from dying to serious but stable.

2. Know where to find trusted information.

After a doctor or other medical personnel has taken care of the most immediate health threats, she can step back, take a deep breath, gather her wits and start thinking of the next steps. You can do the same thing. If this book is handy (carry it with you in your pack or first aid kit), you'll want to consult it to see what to do next. Doctors consult sources all the time—books, online articles and colleagues.

No matter how smart a doctor is, it's impossible to know every detail of what to do in every emergency situation. But a doctor does know the basics, has read about most of the rest and knows where to find the information if he needs to refresh his memory. Take this same approach to learning and practicing first aid.

Don't be intimidated by the wealth of information available about medical emergencies. Find books, hands-on courses, webinars and websites you can trust. Read, watch, listen and do. You can't possibly memorize all the specifics, but the general knowledge will be in the back of your mind. And you'll know the resources to consult when you need to check the details.

Then, keep this book handy. Know where it is. Pack it on your trips. Maybe you'll want to get an extra copy to keep in your cabin or RV.

INITIAL RESPONSE TO MEDICAL EMERGENCIES

There are two vital responses you should perform first in any medical emergency:

1. **Check for potential dangers and hazards to yourself** before you rush in to help the victim. For example, if someone has been electrocuted by a downed wire, you won't help anyone, including yourself, by rushing in without taking precautions so you won't become another victim. Your safety comes first.

2. **Call 911 immediately.** Make this call before you attempt to aid the victim.

THINK LIKE A FIRST RESPONDER: ASSESS THE SITUATION

When you are faced with a medical emergency, follow the same protocol used by first responders to assess the situation:

1. **Call 911.** If other people are around, ask for help and have someone else call 911.

2. **Determine if it is safe for you to help.** For instance, if you help, are you exposing yourself to risk of gunfire, an explosion or traffic? Until you can move the victim to a fairly safe place or reasonably ensure safe surroundings, it's better not to help than to become another accident victim.

3. **If the person is responsive,** ask, "What happened and what hurts?" If you can't rule out trauma, check for a spine injury. Ask him about numbness or tingling in the hands or feet, and ask about neck or back pain. Check the neck and back for injury by pressing on each separate backbone to see if it hurts. If any of these things are positive, you must protect the spine (see page 165).

4. **If the victim is unresponsive,** yell something like, "Hey, are you okay?" or gently shake her or tap her on the chest—anything to get her to respond. If she doesn't, check for breathing and movement. If you find neither, start CPR (see page 39).

5. **If the victim is bleeding badly, do all you can to stop the bleeding.** Use direct pressure first. If that doesn't stop it, use a tourniquet (see page 96).

6. **Visually examine the entire body.** If the person is unresponsive and there's a possibility of trauma or you don't know what

happened, you'll need to visually examine the whole body, which
includes checking under the clothes or taking them off. Check
the victim's eyes to make sure the pupils are the same size.
Shine a light in the eyes to see if the pupils respond to light. If
the pupils are different sizes or don't respond to light in the same
way, suspect severe head trauma.

7. **Clear the spine.** You must be able to rule out a spinal injury
   before moving a person (unless the victim's current position puts
   him in immediate danger—for instance, in traffic or underneath
   falling rocks). For you to "clear the spine":

   - The person must be alert enough to reliably tell you what
     happened. If it was trauma, make sure no area of the spine
     hurts when you apply pressure. Or:

   - You must know, for sure, there was no trauma to the head,
     neck or back—either direct trauma or potential for indirect
     trauma, such as in a fall or vehicle accident.

8. **Protect the spine.** If you cannot rule out an injury to the neck
   or back, you must protect the spine by immobilizing it before
   moving the victim (see page 165).

9. **Get the victim professional help.** If 911 is not available,
   discern whether the person needs immediate transfer to a medical facility and if that is a viable option. If it isn't, you'll need to
   decide how to best handle the situation with what you've got.

ONE

FIRST AID SUPPLIES

This chapter contains suggestions for general medical supplies everyone should have on hand. Some supplies will be for long-term storage, and other suggestions are for use in car kits, day-hiking packs and bug out bags. You will also find tips on how everyday items can be used as alternatives for first aid supplies. Keep this book in your kit for quick reference during an emergency. The suggested quantities found in this chapter are for the minimum amounts you will need. You can increase these quantities depending on your storage area, family size and if you're planning on treating others. You'll also find information on how to acquire special medical supplies, such as prescription medication. I recommend keeping an extra month's worth of any prescription, if possible.

Prevention Tip: Both oral (taken by mouth) and topical (put on the skin) medications (whether over-the-counter or prescription) have expiration dates. A medication loses its effectiveness after its expiration date. Be sure to oc-casionally swap out all the medication in your first aid kits so the expiration date doesn't run out. One way to do this: When you get a fresh supply, take the medicine in storage out for use now and put the fresh supply in storage.

FIRST AID SUPPLIES FOR A LONG-TERM STORAGE AREA

This supply list is ideal for first aid kits you keep in your home and your bug out location.

Elastic Bandages

Minimum: two per family member. The 3-inch (8cm) or 4-inch (10cm) widths are the most versatile.

Notes: Also known as ACE bandages, these bandages will last for several wrappings before the elastic wears out. Wash them if they get dirty. Washing tends to damage the elastic, but they are still usable.

Alternative: Any cloth will do. Tear or fold the cloth into strips that are 3 to 6 inches (8 to 15cm) wide.

Adhesive Bandages

Minimum: at least 100 of the regular size and 25 of the larger ones

Notes: They're also known by the brand name Band-Aids. They make excel-lent sterile dressings for small wounds.

Alternative: gauze or cloth placed in the middle of the sticky side of a strip of tape

HOW TO STERILIZE INSTRUMENTS OR CLOTH

Unless you have your own steam sterilizer, the best method is to boil everything for 20 minutes. Cover the pot with a lid. Using a pressure cooker is also a great sterilization method.

If you can't boil anything, clean away obvious debris and soak the instruments for ten minutes in a povidone-iodine, alcohol, or chlorine solution. If this is not an option, scrub the instruments with any of these solutions or drinking water, and use the cleanest cloth you have available.

If you're using only the tip of a needle or knife, heating it under a flame until red-hot should sterilize that part.

Cotton Balls
Minimum: one package

Notes: Use for small dressings. Great for packing a nosebleed. Add petroleum jelly or antibiotic ointment to make the packing easier to insert and remove. Petroleum-jelly-coated cotton balls also can take the place of kindling to start a fire.

Alternatives: tampons or strips of cloth for nasal packing

Tampons
Minimum: one box

Notes: Use for packing nosebleeds and bullet wounds in addition to feminine hygiene. Can also be used as fire tinder.

Alternative: cloth or gauze

Cotton Tip Applicators, Long Stems
Minimum: box of 100

Notes: Good for applying ointment to small wounds or in nostrils. (Don't use to clean out ears. Doing so irritates the ear canals and tends to pack some wax next to the eardrum, making it difficult to remove.)

Alternative: short-stem cotton tip applicators

Gauze Sponges, Sterile
Minimum: two packs

Notes: Sterile gauze sponges are especially useful for burns because burns are prone to infection, even if you keep them clean.

Alternative: Boil cloth or gauze for 20 minutes. Let dry and use, or keep the dried material in a resealable plastic bag until needed.

Gauze Sponges, Nonsterile
Minimum: two packs (200 per pack)

Notes: The most versatile are the 3 × 3 inch (8cm × 8cm) and 4 × 4 inch (10cm × 10cm) sizes.

Alternative: clean cloth or gauze rolls

Gauze Rolls
Minimum: one roll per person, minimum of four rolls

Notes: Also called Kerlix gauze rolls, these are very versatile: Make a gauze pad by cutting a roll to size and folding to make it thicker. Wrap around a dressing before taping to keep the tape off your skin. Or use it as a wrap to secure a splint.

Alternative: gauze sponges or a clean cloth

Nonstick or Nonadherent Dressing Pads
Minimum: one box

Alternative: Coat one side of regular cloth or gauze with antibiotic ointment or honey. Or use regular gauze or cloth.

QuikClot or Celox Clotting Bandages
Minimum: two packs of the gauze type

Notes: Use only on heavily bleeding wounds that won't stop with direct pressure. Use the gauze style because the granule style is harder to clean from the wound.

Alternative: Apply direct pressure to the wound or a tourniquet or both.

Treatment Tip: Dried blood or tissue fluids can make any dressing stick to a wound. If this happens, soak the stuck dressing in water or peroxide for a few minutes, and it should be easier to remove.

Bandage Scissors
Minimum: two pairs

Notes: Good quality scissors will cut better and last longer.

Alternative: any scissors or knife

Vet Wrap

Minimum: one roll per person

Notes: Also know as Coban, vet wrap is thin, stretchable, self-adherent material that comes in a roll. It can be used in place of tape to hold a bandage in place, to cover large bandages or to wrap around a splint.

Alternative: cloth and tape

Duct Tape

Minimum: two rolls

Notes: Use it to tape bandages and close cuts—and that's just a start. Duct tape has numerous uses in an emergency situation.

Alternative: any type of tape

Paper Tape

Minimum: two rolls

Notes: This is ideal for sensitive skin.

Alternative: wrapping and pinning the dressing in place

Super Glue

Minimum: two tubes

Notes: Use it to cover small nicks, close cuts and help tape stick.

Alternative: any glue

Safety Pins

Minimum: Keep ten to 20 in a small box or pinned to each other.

Notes: Pin bandages or pin a shirttail around an arm for a makeshift sling.

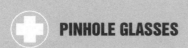

PINHOLE GLASSES

Focusing your vision by looking out of a pinhole can correct near-sightedness to a degree (but studies have shown it won't permanently correct vision). If you lose or damage your corrective glasses or contacts and don't have a spare, you can make a pair of pinhole glasses as a temporary fix.

Remove the damaged lens from your frames and cover the lens area with duct tape (or create frames out of cardboard). Use a safety pin to poke a hole in each duct tape "lens." The holes need to be small but large enough to see out of. When you get the right size, create many additional holes so you'll have a wider field of vision.

Use to pick out splinters, to punch just the right size holes for pinhole glasses (see sidebar) or to stick a hole in a plastic bag or bottle for pressure irrigation.

Alternative: straight pins

SAM Splints
Minimum: two regular size ones, plus one per extra family member; purchase smaller sizes for children

Notes: These are some of the most versatile splints on the market. They're light, and you can cut them to most any size and bend them into most any shape you need.

Alternative: See the "Bones and Joints" chapter on page 162. Sticks, paint stirrers or newspapers secured with wraparound cloth will work. Even a pillow, a coat or any thick material is better than nothing.

Slings
Minimum: one per family member and smaller sizes for children

Notes: They're cheap and lightweight.

Alternative: See the "Bones and Joints" chapter on page 162. Wrap and pin some strong cloth around your arm and neck. A belt can work, or wrap your shirttail around your arm and pin the tail to your shirt.

Tongue Depressors
Minimum: box of 100

Notes: Also called tongue blades; use for looking in throats, applying ointment to wounds and making finger splints.

Alternative: Popsicle sticks

Petroleum Jelly
Minimum: one large container or three smaller ones

Notes: Vaseline is the most common brand name. It can be used to seal chest wounds, keep bandages from sticking, relieve chapped lips and face, and help remove tar or glue from the skin.

Disposable Gloves, Nonsterile
Minimum: four boxes of 100 each

Notes: They reduce the amount of germs getting in a wound and protect the caregiver from any germs in bodily fluids. Consider the vinyl type to avoid latex allergies. Go for one-size-fits-all or the large size. Gloves that are too large are bulky but usable, whereas gloves that are too small are unusable. The cheaper ones work well but may be more likely to tear, in which case just slip a second pair over the first.

Alternative: a pair of dishwashing gloves

Disposable Gloves, Sterile
Minimum: one box of ten pairs

Notes: Save sterile gloves for use on the initial treatment of wounds. These gloves are especially important when tending to wounds that involve broken bones or burns because of the higher risk of infection. It's better to get a size too large than too small.

Syringes
Minimum: five

Notes: The 10ml syringes are handy for irrigating wounds, cleaning out ears and measuring liquid dosages. If you get ones without needles, match them with a box of 1-inch (3cm), 22- or 23-gauge needles for injections, picking out splinters, lancing abscesses, etc. If you get ones with needles, be sure the needles can be removed so you can use only the syringe for irrigation and measuring. Save the needle for future use.

Bulb Syringes
Minimum: one adult size and one child size

Notes: good for irrigating wounds and ears

14-gauge, two-inch (5cm) long Hollow Needles
Minimum: two

Notes: Use to treat someone who has a tension pneumothorax (caused by a collapsed lung, see page 170) and needs air pressure released from the chest. Use with a syringe to drain fluid from the abdomen or chest.

Intravenous (IV) Catheters
Minimum: two 14- or 16-gauge; several smaller ones (18- to 22-gauge) if you plan to start IVs

Notes: Use these in many of the same ways you use a hollow needle. You can pull the needle out and keep the flexible plastic catheter in place. Angiocath is a popular brand.

Blankets
Minimum: one per person

Notes: Thermal reflective blankets are lighter for travel. Blankets are a must to prevent hypothermia, to which trauma victims are especially susceptible.

Paracord
Minimum: 16 feet (5m) of 550-lb. (250kg) Paracord

Notes: Use to secure a splint or make a spine board for neck and back injuries or a makeshift stretcher. Unravel the finer threads and you have some strong string. You can purchase survival bracelets/straps woven out of one continuous length (typically several feet) of Paracord. I recommend having a minimum of two survival bracelets on hand.

Matches and Lighters
Minimum: two matchboxes or more in a waterproof container, along with several lighters

Notes: These may be needed to sterilize instruments or to start a fire to boil water.

Alternative: commercial flint and steel firestarter sets

Thermometers
Minimum: two

Notes: Any oral type (digital, non-mercury, etc.) will do.

Tweezers
Minimum: one regular size and one with thin tips (needle nose)

Notes: The needle nose, especially, is great for removing ticks. Grab the tick by its head and pull steadily and firmly.

Headlamp
Minimum: one, with extra batteries

Notes: This provides an excellent hands-free light source.

Thick Plastic Jar with Lid
Minimum: one

Notes: Use it to store any used sharp items that have been contaminated with blood or pus until you can properly dispose of them. You'll need to take the jar to a place that disposes of medical waste or, if that's not available, burn the jar.

LONG-TERM SUPPLIES THAT REQUIRE TRAINING

Store the following first aid supplies only if you or someone in your party knows how to use them. These supplies won't do you any good and will only take up your valuable storage space if you don't know how to use them.

Blood Pressure Cuff
Minimum: one manual cuff

Notes: For home use consider an automatic one (though the cuff on a manual one can also be used as a tourniquet or temporary pressure dressing). The cuff designed for use on the arm tends to be more accurate than the one designed for the wrist. Check its accuracy ahead of time by letting a trained person check your blood pressure with his manual cuff, then your automatic one.

Treatment Tip: Some people have normal, perfectly healthy blood pressure readings that are well below 120/80 (the very general guideline for a normal reading). In an emergency situation, this type of person might be misdiagnosed as being in shock, so know what your normal blood pressure is ahead of time. Of course, you should also make sure you get treated if your blood pressure runs high when you're at rest.

Pulse Oximeter
Minimum: one

Notes: Clip this around your fingertip (no needles, no blood) and it tells you the oxygen saturation in your blood. When you're injured or sick, this helps clue you in on what may be causing a shortness of breath. If the reading is low, that means your lungs aren't functioning correctly. Just like checking your blood pressure, it's good to know what your normal oxygen saturation is. If you have healthy lungs, it's probably going to be 96 percent or above. So, if you have a fever and maybe a slight cough, a lower-than-normal oxygen saturation gives you a clue that you may have pneumonia. If you've injured your chest or suddenly start having pain when you breathe, a low reading suggests you may have a bruised lung or a pneumothorax (collapsed lung). If the reading gets to around 90 percent or below, you'd better get some supplemental oxygen or get proper treatment fast. On the other hand, if you're short of breath and your oxygen saturation is close to 100 percent, that clues you in that your lungs are functioning fine. Perhaps you're hyperventilating from an anxiety or panic attack.

Stethoscope
Minimum: one

Notes: A cheap one that has one tube instead of two is more than adequate for listening to the heart and lungs and for taking blood pressure.

Alternative: If you don't have one, you can always place your ear on the chest.

Oral Airway (Oropharyngeal Airway)
Minimum: two adult and two children's sizes

Notes: This device keeps the back of the tongue from obstructing the airway of an unconscious person. The best way to learn how to use one is to take a CPR class. See page 44 for more information.

Foley Catheter
Minimum: two; consider having more on hand if anyone in your family has problems urinating or if you may need to treat older people

Notes: For people who can't urinate, Foley catheters are threaded through the urethra (urinary bladder opening) to allow the bladder to empty. Also, they may be used to stop nosebleeds too far up the nose for normal packing. "French" is the name of the unit measurement for these catheters. The usual adult size is a 14 or 16 French.

Intravenous (IV) Fluid
Minimum: one box of one-liter bags of normal saline or lactated Ringer's solution, along with IV tubing and IV catheters or butterfly needles

Medical Staple Gun and Staple Remover
Minimum: two guns and two staple removers

Notes: Each gun should contain ten to 40 staples. A medical staple gun is easier to use than sutures.

Suture Holder and Small Scissors
Minimum: two of each

Notes: Suture holders can be reused after they are cleaned and sterilized.

Suture Material: 3-0 and 4-0 Nylon
Minimum: several packages of both sizes

Notes: Be sure you get the suture material that has the needle attached.

Disposable Sterile Drapes
Minimum: one box

Notes: Use these to cover the area around where you are suturing and to create a sterile place on which to lay your instruments and suture. Some drapes come with a hole (fenestrated) so you can get to the wound. With others, just tear a hole.

Alternative: a clean cloth

Scalpels
Minimum: one box of size 15 or 10

Notes: Use for lancing wounds or cutting off lesions.

DISINFECTANTS

Peroxide
Minimum: two pints

Bleach
Minimum: one gallon

Notes: Warning: Bleach is highly corrosive in the concentrated form. Protect your eyes and skin when handling it. Bleach can be used for disinfecting drinking water (see page 57).

To sanitize instruments, counters, etc., add 1 tablespoon (15ml) of bleach to a gallon (3.7L) of water, and allow the instruments to soak at least ten minutes.

Alternative: Calcium hypochlorite. To disinfect drinking water with this, see page 57. For counters or instruments, make a bleach solution from the calcium hypochlorite, then mix it with water. To make the bleach solution, mix 1 heaping teaspoon (5g) of the calcium hypochlorite granules into 2 gallons (7.6L) of water. Allow it to sit at least 30 minutes. (The solution stays good for a couple of weeks.) Mix one part of the solution to nine parts water. For example, add 1½ ounces (9 teaspoons; 45ml) to each quart (liter) of water. Use in a spray bottle if available.

Rubbing (Isopropyl) Alcohol
Minimum: two pints

Alternative: alcohol pads, one box

Betadine (Povidone-Iodine) 10 Percent Solution

Minimum: one pint to one gallon (½L to 7.6L)

Notes: You can use Betadine to protect your thyroid in place of potassium iodine tablets if radioactive iodide becomes a threat from something such as a nearby nuclear reactor leak. In this case, paint 1½ teaspoons (7ml) on the chest or abdomen daily. For directions on how to use Betadine to disinfect water, see page 55.

Alternative: Betadine (povidone-iodine) pads

Treatment Tip: Keep medications stored in a cool, dry place. Temperature extremes can alter their potency.

OVER-THE-COUNTER MEDICINES

Before using any of these medications, carefully read the precautions, interactions and dosages. Always keep the packaging and instructions with the medication. Have liquid or chewable versions for children.

- **ibuprofen** (Advil, Aleve) or acetaminophen (Tylenol) for pain and fever relief

- **diphenhydramine** (Benadryl) for allergies or to use as a sleep aid

- **ranitidine** (Zantac), famotidine (Pepcid) or your favorite antacid for heartburn and acid reflux

- **loperamide** (Imodium) for diarrhea

- **potassium iodide** tablets to protect the thyroid from radioactive iodine

- **pyrantel pamoate** for pinworms

Topicals (For the Skin)

- lidocaine gel for numbing

- hydrocortisone 1 percent cream for itchy, noninfectious rashes

- aloe vera (bottle or live plant) for soothing burns and irritated skin

- antibacterial ointment (Neosporin, triple antibiotic or bacitracin)

- tea tree oil for poison ivy, lice and scabies, along with antifungal and antibacterial use

- clove oil for toothaches

- permethrin 1 percent, or pyrethrin plus piperonyl butoxide, for head lice

- permethrin 5 percent for scabies

Nasal Inhalers
Minimum: one

Notes: A nasal decongestant can constrict blood vessels and help control nosebleeds. A brand name example is Afrin.

Treatment Tip: Will a doctor really give you extra antibiotics? Some health-care providers might provide you with prescriptions for a few of the medications listed in this chapter if you assure them you'll use the medicines only in dire circumstances and if there comes a time when you don't have access to expert medical care.

PRESCRIPTION ANTIBIOTICS

For all of these medications, carefully read the precautions, interactions and dosages and, of course, go by your health-care provider's recommendations. You must have a prescription to get these.

For Skin Infections, Bronchitis, Pneumonia, Sinus Infections, Ear Infections and Strep Throat

- **Azithromycin** (Z-Pak) is an antibiotic that also treats the sexually transmitted infection chlamydia. Alternatives are clarithromycin (Biaxin) and generic erythromycin.

- **Amoxicillin** is a great drug if you're not allergic to penicillin, but many bacteria, such as staph, have become resistant to it.

- **Cephalexin** is also a good, broad-spectrum antibiotic, but in rare cases, people allergic to penicillin can be allergic to this.

- **Ciprofloxacin** (Cipro) may cause abnormalities in anyone whose bones are still growing (typically 18 years old and under). Don't use if pregnant. It can weaken tendons to the point of rupturing during strenuous activities. Ciprofloxacin is not good for strep throat.

- **Septra and Bactrim** are the same antibiotic (trimethoprim/sulfamethoxazole) with different names. It's one of the only oral antibiotics that is effective against methicillin-resistant Staphylococcus aureus (MRSA). Do not use if you are pregnant. Also, it may make your skin more sensitive to the sun. Not good for strep throat.

For Skin Infections (Antibiotic Ointments)

- **Mupirocin** (Bactroban) is a prescription ointment or cream that actively kills bacteria, even MRSA. (The over-the-counter antibacterial ointments help prevent infections but don't actively kill bacteria.)

FIRST AID SUPPLIES

- **Silver sulfadiazine** (Silvadene) is especially good for burns. It's a sulfa medication, so don't use it if you're allergic to sulfa.

For Urinary Tract Infections, Prostatitis

- **ciprofloxacin,** which also treats gonorrhea
- **Septra and Bactrim** (trimethoprim/sulfamethoxazole)

For Rocky Mountain Spotted Fever and Lyme Disease

- **Doxycycline** may make your skin more sensitive to the sun. Don't use in children under age eight (because it can permanently stain children's teeth) or if pregnant except in extreme emergencies.

For Gastroenteritis (Infectious Diarrhea)

Antibiotics will help only the most severe bacterial diarrhea infections. In fact, rather than help, they can prolong the symptoms. If the infection causes high fever and makes the person very sick, Septra, Bactrim and ciprofloxacin are alternatives.

- **Metronidazole** treats the waterborne parasite giardia.

Treatment Tip: What if you can't get antibiotics? Many infections, such as most sore throats and gastrointestinal infections, are caused by viruses, so antibiotics don't help them anyway. For other infections, such as ones from parasites, fungus or yeast, there are alternative treatments if prescription medications aren't available. For instance, honey is an effective treatment for bacterial skin infections.

HONEY AS A MEDICINE

Honey is an effective alternative to antibacterial ointment. Any type of raw honey will do, but manuka honey and the brand Medihoney have studies to back up their antibacterial properties.

Like antibacterial ointment, honey helps prevent infections. But if you already have a skin infection, honey knocks out the infection better than over-the-counter ointments.

Honey is also great for coughs. To use as a cough suppressant administer:

- ages two to five: ½ teaspoon (3ml) at bedtime
- ages six to 11: 1 teaspoon (5ml) at bedtime
- ages 12 and older: 2 teaspoons (10ml) at bedtime.

Warning: Don't give honey to children under age two. Honey can contain a few botulism spores. While there aren't enough spores to harm older children and adults, there are enough to harm children under two because of their small size.

For Parasitic Infections

- **Ivermectin** kills many intestinal worm infections, including pinworms. It also kills scabies and body, pubic and head lice. Don't take if pregnant or breastfeeding or under age six.

PRESCRIPTION MEDICINES FOR ALLERGIC REACTIONS

Before using prescription allergy medicines, read and know the potential side effects, drug interactions and proper dosages and, of course, follow your health-care provider's recommendations.

- **Injectable epinephrine** is first-line treatment against severe allergic reactions. The brand EpiPen automatically injects epinephrine just underneath the skin. For children, there's the smaller-dose EpiPen Jr. Be sure to read the directions and know how to use it before you need it.

- **Oral steroids** such as prednisone, dexamethasone and several others are good as second-line treatment for a life-threatening allergic reaction and first-line treatment against less severe reactions. Steroids can be combined with epinephrine and antihistamines. However, they can make existing stomach problems or diabetes worse.

- **Antihistamines** such diphenhydramine (the best) or the nonsedating types are another second-line treatment for a life-threatening allergic reaction and first-line treatment for less severe reactions. Antihistamines can be combined with epinephrine and steroids. They can make you drowsy and can cause trouble with urination if there is already some underlying problem, such as an enlarged prostate.

FIRST AID FOR BUG OUT BAG AND HIKING KITS

A first aid kit is an important part of a bug out bag. This packing list reflects the space and weight limitations the bag presents. Download a copy of this list at livingreadyonline.com/pocketfirstaid. You can't carry everything, but with some key supplies, hopefully you will be able to wait it out for help to arrive or make it to a location with more medical supplies. You can also use this list to assemble a first aid kit for hiking trips and other outdoor excursions. See the previous pages for details on how to use the following supplies. The minimal suggested quantity follows each item.

- [ ] elastic bandages, two
- [ ] adhesive bandages, 20
- [ ] SAM Splint, two
- [ ] sling, one
- [ ] bandage scissors, one
- [ ] knife, one
- [ ] Kerlix, four rolls (or use gauze sponges)
- [ ] sterile dressing pads, two
- [ ] QuikClot or Celox, one roll
- [ ] lighters, two
- [ ] duct tape, one large roll
- [ ] safety pins, ten
- [ ] tampons, two
- [ ] disposable gloves, anywhere from a few to a box
- [ ] syringes, two
- [ ] sterile needles, two
- [ ] thermometer, one
- [ ] 14-gauge, 2-inch-long (5cm) hollow needle or comparable-size IV catheter, one
- [ ] thermal reflective blanket, one
- [ ] Paracord survival bracelets, two
- [ ] needle nose tweezers, one
- [ ] headlamp with extra batteries, one
- [ ] Betadine, individually wrapped pads, 20
- [ ] ibuprofen or acetaminonphen, one bottle or several single-dose packets
- [ ] ranitidine (Zantac) or famotidine (Pepcid), one bottle or several packets
- [ ] loperamide (Imodium), one bottle or several packets

Pack the following in resealable bags or other waterproof containers:

- [ ] Medihoney, one jar
- [ ] hydrocortisone 1 percent cream, one tube
- [ ] aloe vera, one bottle
- [ ] antibacterial ointment, one tube
- [ ] clove oil, one bottle
- [ ] tea tree oil, one bottle
- [ ] petroleum-jelly-covered cotton balls
- [ ] super glue, one tube
- [ ] nasal decongestant inhaler, one

Pack these items only if you or someone in your group knows how to use them:

- ☐ blood pressure cuff
- ☐ stethoscope
- ☐ pulse oximeter
- ☐ oropharyngeal airway

Prevention Tip: When a disaster starts, you may not be at home or able to get to your home immediately. Create smaller versions of your bug out bags, containing the things you deem most important, and keep them in your cars (a vehicle kit) and at your place of work (a get-home bag).

IMMUNIZATIONS

Staying up-to-date with your immunizations is a good way to avoid the risk of specific diseases caused by dirty wounds or contaminated food and water (both common scenarios in survival situations). Some people despise the idea of any immunizations and think they do more harm than good. Even so, you might want to read this section for the alternatives (although they are not as effective).

Tetanus

The immunization: A booster is required every ten years. Usually the shot is a combination of tetanus and diphtheria (a dangerous throat infection that can be treated with antibiotics). Sometimes, a vaccine for pertussis (whooping cough) is added to the mix.

The disease: The tetanus bacteria is found in dirt, dust and manure. Always clean wounds thoroughly to decrease your risk. The tetanus disease can be treated with antibiotics and hospitalization, but even then about 10 percent of people who contract tetanus die from the disease. Without treatment, it's fatal about 25 percent of the time. Often, muscle spasms in the throat cut off oxygen, which causes brain damage.

Hepatitis A

The immunization: This is a series of two vaccines. Childhood vaccinations started around 1996. If you didn't receive it, you can still be vaccinated at any age.

The disease: You typically come down with hepatitis A about two to six weeks after ingesting food or water contaminated with feces. It affects your liver and often makes you sick for several weeks with jaundice and flu-like symptoms. Treatment is rest and fluids. After the illness, you're no longer contagious. (While you have it, it can be passed on through your feces in the same way you got it.) Death is a real risk but uncommon.

Hepatitis B

The immunization: This is a series of three vaccines. Childhood vaccinations started around 1991. If you didn't receive it, you can still be vaccinated at any age.

The disease: You come down with this virus about three months after contaminated blood gets in an open wound. It can also be transmitted in semen. The initial symptoms of the illness are similar to those of hepatitis A. In some people (not everyone), the virus never leaves, and they're contagious for life. These people have a higher risk for eventual death from cirrhosis of the liver.

TWO

RESUSCITATION

This chapter teaches you what to do when a person suddenly collapses. You may or may not know what caused the person to collapse. Either way, there is standard protocol that you can follow to help the victim.

WHAT TO DO WHEN A PERSON COLLAPSES

Here is the suggested protocol for helping someone who has collapsed:

1. Direct someone to call 911. If you're alone, make the call yourself.

2. If the victim is awake or moving, the person must have circulation, so do not start chest compressions.

3. If the victim seems unconscious, loudly ask, "Are you okay?" If there's no response, shake the person and yell again. If there's still no response and the person is not moving and doesn't appear to be breathing, ensure the victim is flat on his back with a hard surface underneath and start chest compressions.

4. Check for a pulse only if you know how to do so properly. Using the wrong technique will give you incorrect results.

5. If you're in a public place, direct someone to look for an AED (automatic external defibrillator, required by law). If one is available, immediately open it and follow the instructions.

HOW TO PERFORM CHEST COMPRESSIONS

1. Kneel beside the person with both of your knees close to the person's chest. Lean over the chest.

2. Place your hands on top of each other and position the base of your bottom hand over the middle part of the breastbone. Position your elbows and shoulders directly over your hands.

3. Use your weight to compress the chest, leaning your entire body weight down on your arms to apply pressure. Do not bend your elbows (like they do on TV). Compress the chest down at least 2 inches (5cm; yes, that's also a lot more than they do on TV).

4. Compress at a minimum rate of 100 times per minute. The rate is the same as the beat of the Bee Gees' tune "Stayin' Alive."

RESUSCITATION

5. Compress until help arrives. If you're using an AED, it will direct you when to compress and when to stop.

6. If you don't have an AED, stop and quickly recheck for a pulse or other signs of life such as breathing or responsiveness every two minutes. If someone is with you, take turns performing compressions.

7. If no help comes and you don't get a pulse or other sign of life, there will come a time when continuing is fruitless. Stop if you become exhausted. It's extremely rare to revive a person unless you have an AED or can transfer her to a medical facility. Even then, it's pretty uncommon, so don't be too hard on yourself if you've done your best.

Treatment Tip: A precordial thump is a technique in which you sharply hit the middle of the person's chest with the side of your fist to shock the heart back into beating. It once was part of the usual regimen of CPR but has been found to be not worth the effort if you have an AED or expert help on the way. However, if you're on your own, it's worth a try and occasionally (although, again, rarely) works.

BREATHING

The American Heart Association and others currently recommend that in most situations, nonmedical personnel shouldn't spend too much time figuring out whether a collapsed person is breathing. Studies show that time is better spent starting immediate chest compressions and employing an AED than listening to the chest, watching for chest movement or holding a hand near the mouth and nose. The assumption is that if a person has collapsed and is unresponsive, odds are his heart and breathing have stopped.

Note that "agonal" breathing should be treated the same way as not breathing at all. Agonal breathing is the occasional (usually every ten seconds or less), irregular reflex gasp performed by someone whose heart has stopped.

When to Check for Breathing

Check for breathing in cases of:

- drowning

- severe hypothermia (see page 75)

- suspected head trauma

- drug overdose

- the victim is a baby

How to Check for Breathing

Do these steps as quickly as possible:

1. Watch the chest for movement caused by breathing. If you're not sure whether you see any, place your ear on the chest and listen. Do this for no longer than five to ten seconds.

2. If there's no breathing or there's troubled breathing, check the airway by swiping two fingers over the tongue and back of the throat. Remove any foreign objects, including dentures. Be sure to swipe and not push so any foreign object does not move farther back in the throat.

3. Recheck for breathing.

4. If there's still no breathing or there's troubled breathing, try one of the following techniques for repositioning the airway:

   - If you're sure there's been no head or neck trauma, grab both sides of the face and tilt the head backward.

   - If you can't rule out head or neck trauma, kneel at the head of the victim. Place your hands on either side of the head to keep it still. Place your thumbs on each side of the jaw below the ears. Using only your thumbs, push the lower jaw outward.

5. Recheck for breathing.

How to Assist a Victim with Breathing

If you've done steps one through five and there's still no breathing, or if the respirations are six per minute or fewer, try the following steps.

If you have a commercial barrier device, such as a CPR mask, use it to protect yourself from the victim's fluids. If not, consider putting a large hole in any waterproof covering, such as exam gloves or a plastic bag, and placing it between your mouth and the victim's.

1. Kneel next to the victim. Pinch her nose shut, seal your mouth over hers and blow a puff of air just strong enough to make her chest rise.

2. If the chest doesn't rise, recheck the airway, reposition the head and jaw, and check for breathing. If none, repeat step one.

3. After two more puffs, check for a pulse or signs of life. If none can be found, start chest compressions as described on page 39.

4. After two minutes of chest compressions, do one of the following:

   - If there is a pulse but no breathing: Repeat breaths about every five seconds (12 per minute) without chest compressions.

   - If there is no pulse: Give two breaths, then 30 chest compressions. Continue repeating this breaths/compressions cycle until expert help arrives or until you become exhausted.

ENSURING AN OPEN AIRWAY

Whether a person is breathing on his own or you're assisting the breathing, an open airway is essential. A foreign object (including vomit) or the victim's tongue can block the airway. No, you never "swallow your tongue," but when you're unconscious or semiconscious, your muscles are so relaxed that the back of the tongue can block the throat. Chest compressions and breathing for a victim can cause the victim to vomit.

How to Keep an Airway Open if There Is No Head or Neck Trauma

1. Grab both sides of the victim's face and tilt the head backward.

2. Turn the victim on his side. Turn both his body and head. Then bend his knees and place his top leg in front of the bottom one and prop something behind his back to keep him on his side. In this position, the tongue usually moves away from the back of the throat, and vomit can drain out of the mouth rather than down the windpipe.

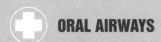 # ORAL AIRWAYS

Oral airways (also known as oropharyngeal airways) are commercial devices you insert into the mouth to keep the tongue from blocking the airway. Insert this curved device between the roof of the mouth and the tongue with the tip pointed upward toward the victim's face. Gently but firmly push it in until only the last part is still sticking out of the mouth. Then turn it until the tip is facing downward, toward the throat.

It's important that you know ahead of time the proper size to use and how to insert it. Ask a health-care provider to demonstrate its use.

Insert the airway as quickly as possible to decrease the chances of the person vomiting during the process. No matter how fast you are, after the oral airway is inserted, turn the person on his side unless there's a reason not to, such as chest compressions or potential head or neck trauma.

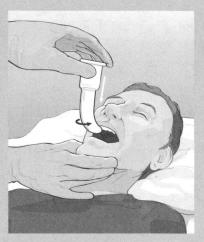

Take a CPR class to learn how to properly insert an oral airway.

How to Keep an Airway Open if There Is Head or Neck Trauma

See page 167 for instructions on moving someone with a spine injury.

1. If you can't turn the victim on her side, use an oral airway (see the sidebar).

2. If you don't have an oral airway, use a piece of dry cloth to grab the tip of the tongue and gently pull.

3. As a last resort, if the victim is unconscious, you can keep the tongue pulled out by safety pinning it to the lower lip.

CHOKING

Choking occurs when a conscious person gets something—usually food—stuck in his throat, blocking the airway. Usually the person can dislodge the food by coughing. But if the object blocks the airway long enough, the person could die.

Signs of Choking

- hand grasping the throat with a panicked look on her face

- no sounds, including coughing or talking, coming from the person

- face turning red or blue

How to Treat Choking

Call 911 if available. Before you do anything else, if the person is conscious, ask, "Are you choking?" If the answer appears to be yes, ask, "Can I help?" Doing otherwise could legally be considered battery. However, this doesn't apply if the person is unconscious or can't respond. If the person gives you approval to help and is standing or sitting, you can attempt abdominal thrusts (Heimlich maneuver).

How to Perform Abdominal Thrusts

1. Get behind the person and encircle your arms around the waist.

2. Place the base of one of your hands at the top of the abdomen. Or make a fist above the navel and below the rib cage. (If the person is pregnant or too large for this, place your fist at the middle of the breastbone.)

3. Grab your positioned hand with your other hand.

4. Squeeze sharply with all the pressure going through your hand and onto the abdomen or chest.

5. If the victim doesn't improve by gasping for air, repeat this maneuver until she does.

How to Help a Choking Victim Who Has Collapsed

1. Kneel beside the victim on the floor. Position the base of one of your hands between the navel and rib cage. (If the person is pregnant, position your hand at the middle of her breastbone.)

2. Place the base of your other hand on top of your positioned one.

3. Push down sharply. Angle the push toward the chest.

4. If the person is unconscious, swipe two fingers in the mouth to check for and remove any foreign object.

5. Repeat this procedure until the person is breathing.

How to Help a Choking Infant or Toddler

1. Take the baby in your arms and position the head downward. Often this can be done single-handedly by resting the baby on his belly on your forearm.

2. Sharply slap between the shoulder blades with the heel (base) of your hand. Repeat as needed, up to five times.

3. Check the mouth and remove any foreign objects.

4. If the baby is still not breathing, turn the baby on his back. Place two fingertips at mid-chest and sharply push. Repeat as needed, up to five times.

5. Check the mouth and remove any foreign objects.

6. Alternate the back slaps and chest thrusts as long as needed.

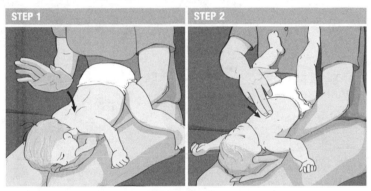

Proper technique to dislodge an object from a choking baby.

THREE

WATER AND HYDRATION

No matter where you are or what you're doing, you're not going to make it far without water. It keeps your heart pumping, your blood flowing and your mind functioning. It's even required to keep your body from getting too hot or too cold. In fact, water affects every cell in your body. Prevention is the best treatment for any ailment. Stay well hydrated and you'll never need to worry about treating dehydration.

WATER REQUIREMENTS FOR PROPER HYDRATION

An adult at rest needs an average of 2 quarts (2L) of water a day—more in dry climates. And if you're fairly active, your body can easily use up a quart (liter) of water every hour or two.

Children have more skin surface area per pound (kilogram) of body weight, so they lose proportionally more water through their skin surface than adults lose. So they need more water in proportion to their body mass than an adult does, even though they don't consume as much water as an adult.

HOW MUCH WATER

PERSON	MINIMUM AMOUNT OF DRINKING WATER PER DAY	MINIMUM AMOUNT OF WASHING WATER PER DAY
Adults and children weighing over 44 lbs (20 kg)	2 quarts (2 liters)	2 quarts (2 liters)
Children under 44 lbs (20 kg)	100 milliliters per kilogram for first 10 kg of body weight. 50 ml per kilogram for next 10 kg	2 quarts (2 liters)

Additional Water Needs

In addition to drinking water, you need water to bathe, wash your hands, clean wounds, wash utensils, etc. To prevent illness, all of the water you use for hygiene and washing needs to be clean enough to drink.

You can never have too much water on hand. In an emergency, 1 gallon (4L) a day per person is about the minimum you need for hydration and hygiene. You'll need much more if you're going to be active.

**BASIC FLUID REQUIREMENTS
FOR CHILDREN**

It's easiest to calculate how much water a child needs using the
metric system (kilograms and milliliters) and convert your findings
into standard units (pounds and ounces) if you need to. So first,
know your metrics:

- A kilogram (kg) is 2.2 pounds (lbs).

- About 30 milliliters (ml) equal 1 ounce (oz).

- 1,000 milliliters (ml) equal about 1 quart.

A child needs the following amount of water per day:

- 100ml per kilogram for the first 10kg of body weight. That
  means a child who weighs 10kg (22 lbs) is going to need
  1,000ml (33⅓ oz) per day. That's about a quart.

- 50ml per kilogram for the next 10kg (22 lb) of body weight.
  That means a 20kg (44 lb) child is going to need about
  1½ quarts (1½L) per day (1 quart for the first 22 lbs and
  ½ quart for the next 22 lbs).

- If the child weighs more than 44 lbs (20kg), let's just make
  it 2 quarts (2L) per day.

Just like adults, children will need more water if they are especially
active or in a dry climate.

Carry an adequate amount of water with you any time you head out for an activity that will take you away from drinkable water for several hours. Having water on hand is your best defense against dehydration.

Water weighs about 8 pounds per gallon (4kg per 3.8L). Use multiple containers to distribute the load evenly if you're carrying it. Make sure everyone in your group carries enough water to meet his own hydration needs.

Water Containers

Whenever you need to carry water with you or store water ahead of time, it's a good idea to use at least two different kinds of containers for the following reasons:

- You have a backup container in case one breaks.

- You can evenly distribute the weight of the water if you're carrying it.

- If you need to source water from nature, you can reduce the odds of contamination by designating one container for collecting the water and the other container for treating the water.

Water containers come in a number of styles—metal, hard plastic, collapsible, backpack. These features are helpful:

- **Heat and fire resistant:** A metal container is most likely to meet this requirement. A fire-resistant container gives you something to boil water in should the need arise.

- **Marked to indicate liquid measurements** (such as 500ml or 16oz): These measurements will help you accurately use chemical treatments on the water.

- **Collapsible:** These containers weigh practically nothing when empty and can fold up incredibly small, making them easy to carry as backup containers.

When treating water sourced from nature, be sure to thoroughly clean the rim and drinking spout of a water container with drinkable water before drinking out of it. Contaminated water may have splashed onto these surfaces, leaving behind germs that could make you sick.

CONSERVING THE WATER YOU HAVE

If drinkable water is in short supply, preserve what you have by:

- cleaning wounds with peroxide, rubbing alcohol (warning: it burns) or even the kind of alcohol you drink

- washing your hands with waterless soap or wearing gloves, or doing both

- limiting water loss from your body

Prevention Tip: Hydrate yourself by drinking around ½ quart (½L) of water before you start your activity. You tend to absorb water more efficiently before you start moving than after you've started working or walking. Follow this practice and you'll get a good start on preventing dehydration.

Limiting Water Loss From Your Body

Your body loses water mainly through urination and sweating. To reduce urination, avoid drinking caffeine, tea and alcohol.

To reduce sweating in hot weather, stay in the shade, do your heaviest activities in the cool of the day, and rest for up to 20 minutes for every 40 minutes you are active.

To reduce sweating in cold weather, layer your clothes and remove a layer before you get warm enough to sweat.

You also lose water when you breathe (you expel some of the moisture lining your airways). Reduce this by moderating your physical activity level so you don't exert enough energy to start breathing hard. You also won't break a sweat.

THE TYPE OF WATER IS IMPORTANT

Not any old water will do. Water that your body can use to continue functioning needs to meet three criteria:

1. **It needs to be fresh.** Seawater won't cut it, unless you know how to desalinate (take the salt out of) it. And contrary to popular media, your urine isn't a viable option either. Both seawater and urine contain concentrations of too many other ingredients that pull water out of your body. They actually dehydrate you faster than if you drink nothing at all.

2. **It needs to be free of germs that can make you sick.** Notice it doesn't necessarily need to be completely germ-free. Many germs in water won't harm your body at all. The harmful germs to worry about include:

   - the protozoa parasites cryptosporidium, giardia and others

   - bacteria such as salmonella, shigella and E. coli

   - various viruses such as hepatitis A

3. **It's ideal to have water free of toxins** such as lead, arsenic, etc.

The germs that make you sick are most often found in water that's been contaminated with feces from humans or animals. Unfortunately, these days, finding an uncontaminated stream, pond or lake is about as likely as finding gold at the end of the rainbow. Even snow and rainwater can't be fully trusted. If you're collecting water directly from a natural source, you must assume it's contaminated with harmful germs.

HOW TO MAKE WATER DRINKABLE

Now there's nothing I know of that's going to get rid of all toxins (activated charcoal may help), but there are several fairly simple ways to get rid of bacteria, viruses and parasites so you won't get sick, at least right away. Making water drinkable is a two-step process:

Step 1. Filter.

Filtering removes large debris and bacteria that's hanging on to larger particles. Potential filters include:

- clean cotton cloth, such as a T-shirt

- bandana or scarf

- coffee filter

- sand

If you don't have a makeshift filter available, let the particles in your container settle to the bottom, and pour off the clear water at the top.

Step 2. Disinfect.

Filtering is not enough. You must treat the water with heat or chemicals to kill the germs in it. With heat or chemical methods, water purification depends on two variables—the intensity (or concentration) of the disinfectant and the amount of time the disinfectant has contact with the germs. In other words, heating water to just under boiling for about 30 minutes probably kills the germs as well as heating it to a rapid boil for one minute. Lower heat requires a longer time to be effective.

You can decrease the concentration of a chemical treatment and still kill the germs by increasing the amount of time the chemicals are in contact with contaminated water. Or you can decrease the amount of time needed to kill the germs by increasing the concentration of the disinfectant used.

Of course, these methods have limits. Diluting the concentration of the chemical too much can ensure the germs don't die no matter how long you wait, and you can add so much chemical that your solution becomes a poison of its own.

WATER DISINFECTION METHOD 1: BOILING

This is the way to go if you have access to enough heat. By the time the water comes to a rolling boil, all the bad bugs should be dead. To be extra safe, keep the water boiling for a full minute, three at the most. If possible, keep the pot covered while boiling so you don't lose water through evaporation. And, for extra safety, keep the lid on the pot for an extra three minutes after the boiling has stopped to reduce the risk of being burned by steam.

Advantages

- You're not adding chemicals.

- It's easy to know how long to treat—to the boiling point.

Disadvantages

- You must have a heat-resistant container.

- You must have fire-starting material and enough fuel.

- You're more quickly depleting valuable heat resources such as wood or other fuels.

WATER DISINFECTION METHOD 2: IODINE

This method is most effective if combined with the microfiltration method described on page 59.

If the water is cloudy or really cold, double the recommended disinfecting time when treating with iodine. For liquid iodine, it helps to have a dropper or syringe.

- **Iodine tablets:** Use as directed from the manufacturer. Be sure to wait the allotted time—usually 30 minutes.

- **Iodine solution** (tincture) 2 percent: 0.4ml (10 drops) per quart (liter) of water and wait 30 minutes, or 0.2ml (5 drops) and wait an hour.

- **Betadine** (povidone-iodine 10 percent) solution: 0.7ml (16 drops) in a quart (liter) of water and wait 30 minutes, or 0.4ml (8 drops) and wait an hour.

Advantages

- Easy to store or carry the tablets.

- A small amount of iodine is needed daily for normal thyroid function anyway.

Disadvantages

- Iodine may not kill all the germs, especially protozoa like cryptococcus and giardia that can protect themselves by forming cysts.

- Taste can be improved by using the lesser concentration (which increases the treatment time) or by adding about 50mg of vitamin C to each quart (liter) of water after the treatment is finished. Don't add the vitamin C before the iodine treatment is finished because it may interfere with the effectiveness of the treatment. (Using flavored tablets that contain vitamin C also works.)

- Iodine stains anything it touches.

- Tablets can lose potency if they get too moist, too hot or too old. (They lose about 8 percent potency in a year.)

- Iodine may cause thyroid problems in a small percentage of people if this large amount is taken for several weeks.

- Some people are allergic to iodine, but severe reactions are rare.

- Pregnant women need daily iodine, but this much can harm the fetus's thyroid.

WATER DISINFECTION METHOD 3: CHLORINE

This works very similarly to iodine. This method is most effective if combined with the microfiltration method described on page 59. Again, double the recommended disinfecting time when treating with chlorine if the water is cloudy or really cold. For liquid chlorine, it helps to have a dropper or syringe.

- **Sodium hypochlorite** (household bleach 5 percent): 0.2ml (4 drops) per quart (liter) of water for 30 minutes, or 0.1ml (2 drops) for an hour.

- **Calcium hypochlorite** $\frac{1}{10}$ gram tablet: ¼ tablet in 2 quarts (2L) of water for 30 minutes.

- **Calcium hypochlorite granules:** This is a two-step process:

    1. Mix one heaping teaspoon (5g) of the granules into 2 gallons (8L) of water to make a bleach solution. The bleach solution stays good for a couple of weeks.

    2. Mix one part of the bleach solution into 100 parts of water to make a drinkable solution. Let it sit for 30 minutes. Example: To treat 1 quart (1L) of water, add 2 teaspoons (10ml) of the bleach solution; or add 1 pint (470ml) of bleach solution into about 100 pints (12.5 gallons; 47L) of water.

Advantages

- Chlorine is easily accessible.

- The granules are especially cheap and can be stored in the solid form for a long time.

Disadvantages

- The bleach solution may not kill all the germs, especially protozoa like cryptococcus and giardia that can protect themselves by forming cysts.

- Taste can be improved with lesser concentration or mixing 50mg of vitamin C per quart (liter) of water. Add the vitamin C 30 minutes or more after mixing the bleach and water. Using flavored tablets that contain vitamin C also works.

- Household bleach loses its potency in a year or two.

- Mixing the granules correctly takes a little calculating.

- The fumes and solution can irritate your airway, throat and stomach at higher concentrations.

WATER DISINFECTION METHOD 4: UV RAYS

For this method, you need a container with a clear, non-UV-resistant glass cover and a black bottom (or a black surface to set the container on). The water needs at least four hours of direct sunlight and eight hours of sitting time, preferably more of both. Just to be safe, you can combine it with the microfiltration method on page 59.

Advantages

- Easy. No chemicals and no fire to maintain.

- Requires only a container and sunlight.

Disadvantages

- Needs a lot of time and adequate sun.

WATER DISINFECTION METHOD 5: MICROFILTRATION

This process involves a water filter that has holes too small to see—no bigger than 1 micron in diameter. Most protozoa and bacteria are larger than 1 micron, which is why the filter is able to remove them. You can purchase microfilters in a number of styles. Some use a pump to push the water through the filter. Others use suction. Gravity-fed options are also available.

According to the Centers for Disease Control and Prevention (CDC), if the product is approved to get rid of cryptosporidium, it should have one of four messages on the package label:

1. "Reverse osmosis"

2. "Absolute pore size of 1 micron or smaller" (make sure it says *absolute* and not *nominal*)

3. "Tested and certified by NSF Standard 53 or NSF Standard 58 for cyst removal"

4. "Tested and certified by NSF Standard 53 or NSF Standard 58 for cyst reduction"

Advantages

- May work better than chemicals on cysted parasites like cryptosporidium and giardia.

- Microfilters designed for backpacking are highly portable.

- There's no treatment time. As soon as the water comes through the filter, it's ready to drink. So you can fill a water bottle with drinkable water nearly as fast as a faucet.

Disadvantages

- The filters are relatively expensive.

- There are a lot of false claims about the effectiveness of microfilters. Even a 1 micron hole is way too large for viruses and some bacteria. So filtration is best combined with one of the other above methods for maximum effectiveness.

DEHYDRATION

Getting thirsty and having a dry mouth are not reliable early indicators of dehydration because they're so subjective. Some people get thirsty after a few minutes of activity; others take a lot longer. An increased pulse rate is also hard to use reliably because exercise normally can raise your heart rate to 120 or 130 beats per minute.

On the other hand, if you wait for late signs like decreased sweat production, confusion or disorientation, you've waited too long. Things are getting serious. Fortunately, there is an easy and more reliable way to help you recognize dehydration before you get to that point: checking your urine concentration (see the sidebar).

URINE CONCENTRATION

If you understand what you're looking for, the color and darkness of your urine can be a reliable indicator of early dehydration.

Start taking note of your normal urine color. It's usually a light yellow, even clear if you've been drinking a lot of fluids. When you start getting dehydrated, your kidneys try to conserve the water in your body by not putting out as much water with the other waste materials. Your urine becomes more concentrated and takes on a darker yellow color. In general, the darker yellow the urine, the more dehydrated you are.

When your urine becomes darker, it's time to drink a little more water. You'll know you're drinking enough when the urine becomes light yellow again.

Some medications, including vitamins, discolor your urine and will invalidate the method of measuring for dehydration. Liver disease and sometimes bladder infections can also do this.

Symptoms of Moderate to Severe Dehydration

- headaches

- dizziness

- extreme fatigue

- resting heart rate over 100 beats per minute (you'll need to know what's normal for yourself)

- decreased urination

Treating Dehydration

Water is great. Can't beat it. Sports drinks are just as good and, due to taste, may be easier to drink in large quantities.

If you have no other choice and clean water is not an option, just drink the cleanest fresh water available. Yes, you're likely to get diarrhea, but that's usually many hours away if caused by bacteria, and days to weeks away if caused by protozoa. You may have to deal with your immediate concern, which is staying alive now, and worry about the consequences later—hopefully when you've reached expert medical care.

DEHYDRATION CAUSED BY DIARRHEA AND VOMITING

Antibiotics don't help the diarrhea or vomiting caused by most bacterial or viral infections. The symptoms just have to run their course, which may last for hours or days. Until they do, dehydration is the danger and usual cause of death in this situation. With diarrhea or vomiting, you lose a lot of water and also significant amounts of electrolytes (sodium and potassium).

Types of Oral Rehydration Fluids

- Water is good in these situations, but water with electrolytes and calories is better.

- Pedialyte is ideal for children or adults.

- Sports drinks have too much sugar, which may make the diarrhea worse. Try diluting the drink 1:1 with water.

- Nursing babies can continue breast milk but may need extra fluids to avoid dehydration.

Amount to Drink to Avoid Dehydration with Diarrhea

According to the World Health Organization, if you have diarrhea, you should drink the following amounts to avoid dehydration:

- **Children under age two:** ¼ to ½ cup (50–100ml, or 2–3 oz) after each loose stool, up to ½ quart (½ liter) per day.

- **Children ages two to nine:** ½ cup to 1 cup (100–200ml, or 3–7 oz) after each loose stool, up to 1 quart (1L) per day.

- **People age ten and over:** as much as they want, up to 2 quarts (2L) per day, along with regular water.

If the person seems to be getting dehydrated, give up to 1 ounce per pound of body weight (80ml per kilogram) within a four-hour period.

Tips for Keeping Down Liquids If Vomiting

1. **Test your tolerance.** I learned this lesson when I caught a bug in college. A few minutes after vomiting, I'd try swigging some fluids because I was worried about getting dehydrated. I'd vomit them up and drink some more. I was harming myself more than I was help-ing. Every time I vomited, I lost not only what I had drank but also electrolytes such as sodium and potassium from my stomach juices.

2. **Allow your stomach some rest.** Sometimes a rest is all it takes. Wait a few hours. Then start sipping, slowly. For a baby or adult, start with a teaspoon (5ml) at a time. Wait ten minutes and try another. If it doesn't stay down, wait 15 or 20 minutes. After a few times of successfully keeping down a teaspoon (5ml), increase the amount to 2 teaspoons (10ml) at a time, then 14 (20ml).

MAKE YOUR OWN ORAL REHYDRATION FLUID

If you make the following homemade recipe for oral rehydration fluid, be sure to measure the ingredients accurately. Too much sugar will make the diarrhea worse. Too much salt could be dangerous. Preferably use a measuring device. Also note that although the World Health Organization thinks this recipe is the ideal strength, if you have a question of measurement, it's better to make it more diluted than too strong.

Recipe for Homemade Rehydration Salts

For every quart (liter) of water add:

- 6 level teaspoons (30g) of sugar

- ½ teaspoon (2.5g) of salt

This version lacks potassium, so you can mix in about 4 ounces (118ml) of orange juice (if you add juice, reduce the amount of sugar you add by 1 or 2 teaspoons [5 or 10g]) or have a bite of a banana. Or, to each quart of the above, add about ¼ teaspoon (1.25g) of a salt substitute (such as NoSalt) that contains potassium instead of sodium.

At least one study has shown you can substitute up to 10 teaspoons (50ml) of honey for the sugar. Molasses probably works just as well.

3. Don't gulp large amounts. Avoid the temptation, even if you're thirsty. Your stomach tolerates smaller amounts better. Don't test the limits. Remember, vomiting is worse than not drinking at all.

What About Eating?

1. Start back to eating after the diarrhea has calmed down. Many recommend eating whatever you want as tolerated. I'm still a proponent of starting with the BRAT diet. That's Bananas, Rice, Applesauce, Toast (no butter). Plain, boiled potatoes and noodles are also good, but nothing else for 24 hours.

2. Avoid greasy foods and milk (other than breast milk for babies) for several days. Some people, especially children, may be unable to digest cow's milk properly for days, even up to a month, after a bad case of diarrhea.

What About Over-the-Counter Medicines?

They may decrease the diarrhea frequency for a while, but they don't limit the total time you're going to have it. Sometimes they can make it last longer. Consider them if you're planning to get back to better care facilities within 12 hours. Taking Pepto-Bismol for traveler's diarrhea is an exception.

FOUR

EXPOSURE: HYPERTHERMIA AND HYPOTHERMIA

Every second of every day that you are alive, your body produces heat as a result of cell metabolism. If your body didn't have a way to get rid of that heat, your insides would soon cook. But you can't lose all of the heat, or your insides would soon freeze. Fortunately, your body has an efficient system in place that keeps your insides almost always within four degrees of 98.6°F (37°C), the temperature at which your organs work their best.

Your body utilizes your circulatory system and skin as heat conductors, carrying away or conserving the heat your body produces. When your insides sense your core temperature is getting too hot, blood vessels close to your skin dilate, or get bigger, and draw up your hot inner blood so more heat is released through your skin's surface. If your core is in danger of getting too cold, the blood vessels near your skin contract, or get smaller, restricting blood flow near the surface so less heat escapes through your skin. It's a continuous cycle that works well unless the outside air becomes too hot or too cold for too long, which can overwhelm the process. This chapter will help you combat external forces that can cause your body temperature to climb too high (hyperthermia) or fall too low (hypothermia).

DRESS FOR SURVIVAL

Clothing is your first line of defense against external heat and cold (the elements). Always dress appropriately for the weather and carry an extra layer of clothing with you just in case. An 80°F (27°C) afternoon may be followed by a 40°F (4°C) night.

To get the most protection from your clothing, keep these tips in mind:

- Dress in layers and choose loose-fitting cuts.

- Try to include at least one layer of long sleeves and full pants so you can cover all your skin if needed.

- Choose quick-drying fabrics; cotton is breathable but takes a long time to dry.

- Include a hat to protect the top of your head, ears, face and neck.

HYPERTHERMIA (OVERHEATING)

You experience a condition known as hyperthermia when your body gets overheated and your core temperature soars. Hyperthermia is usually caused when the air around you is too hot or your cells are working too hard with exercise and, therefore, producing too much heat. It can also be caused by a combination of hot air temperature and exercise that is too strenuous.

Your body has some tricks to help cope with this heat, but it needs a week or two to best acclimate. After prolonged exposure to a hot climate, your body will adapt to the higher heat in the following ways:

1. Your body sweats more. The sweat cools your skin as it evaporates.

2. Your sweat starts containing a lesser concentration of salt so your body doesn't become depleted of sodium as quickly.

3. Your heart begins to beat more efficiently, circulating more blood per beat to cool at your skin surface.

4. All of your cells become more efficient, making less heat per unit of energy produced.

Unfortunately, sudden heat waves don't give your body time to adapt in these ways. And even if you were to adapt, your coping mechanisms may still not be enough when the air temperature reaches above 90°F (32°C) (close to your core temp). Add a vigorous activity, which increases your metabolism and produces more heat, or high humidity, which prevents your sweat from effectively evaporating off your skin, or both, and you put yourself at a great risk to overheat.

Factors that Increase Your Risk of Overheating

- external air temperature above 90°F (32°C)

- high humidity

- prolonged strenuous physical activity

- age—the elderly and children under age four are particularly susceptible

- chronic illness

Ways to Avoid Becoming Overheated

When temperatures or humidity levels soar, take serious steps to avoid overheating. Here are some tips on how you can do that:

- Drink a noncaffeinated, nonalcoholic beverage every hour. Dehydration makes hyperthermia worse. The beverage doesn't have to be ice-cold. In fact, drinking extremely cold beverages in high heat can cause stomach spasms.

- Increase your fluid intake even more if you are physically active. You may need as much as a quart (liter) or two per hour if you are doing particularly strenuous work.

- Avoid strenuous activity during the hottest part of the day (10 A.M. to 4 P.M.).

- If you are drinking only water, add a ½ teaspoon (2.5g) of salt to the first couple of quarts (liters) you drink per day if you think you'll be sweating profusely. Otherwise, most people get plenty of salt with their food. Caveat: If your doctor has suggested limiting your amount of fluids or salt, get her advice on what to do.

- Limit your intake of caffeine, sugary drinks and alcohol, as they actually dehydrate you.

- Wear loose, breathable clothes.

- Take a midday shower, bath or sponging. Hop in the nearest, and cleanest, lake or stream to cool off.

⊕ SUNBURN

Don't forget to protect yourself against this important and overlooked issue. Not only does too much sun age your skin and increase your risk for certain skin cancers, but it can actually incapacitate you with blisters, swelling and pain, and put you at risk for skin infections.

To protect your skin from sunburn, consider wearing loose, light-colored clothes and a wide-brimmed hat. Apply an SPF 30 sunscreen thickly and evenly to bare-skin areas, and include the nose, cheeks, tops of the ears and any bald spots on your scalp. Unless you're using sunscreen designed for the face, be careful around the eyes because it can cause irritation.

Don't forget the back and front of your neck, any bare part of your chest, the backs of your hands, the tops of your feet and the backs of your legs if you're wearing shorts. Reapply every few hours. Be sure to wear a good pair of sunglasses—the kind that screens out 99 percent-plus of UV rays.

For sunburn treatment, see the burns section in the chapter on skin wounds (page 122).

- If you're going to be in the sun a lot, don't forget to frequently apply sunblock. Also consider wearing a wide-brimmed hat.

- Take frequent breaks in the shade. Fan a little with whatever you have available.

- If you're in a shelter with no air-conditioning, open windows (or the flaps if you're in a tent) and use a fan. Good air ventilation is essential. Note that a fan can't help cool your core if the air it circulates is in the mid-nineties or above. Placing cool water or a bucket of ice in front of the fan can cool the air.

MUSCLE CRAMPING

People sometimes experience muscle cramps when they begin to overheat. The cramps are usually caused by a decrease in sodium in the body. You lose salt whenever you sweat, and profuse sweating can cause you to lose a lot of sodium in a short amount of time, bringing on cramps. Muscle cramping can be an early symptom of heat exhaustion, so take it seriously and treat it.

How to Treat Muscle Cramping

- Rest.

- Massage the muscles.

- Drink an extra quart (liter) or two of a sports drink, or mix ½ teaspoon (2.5g) of salt in a quart (liter) of water. See the sidebar on oral rehydration fluids, page 64, for details.

- Eat a banana or, if you have it, add ¼ teaspoon (1.25g) of potassium to the water.

HEAT EXHAUSTION

Your body functions best at 98.6°F (37°C), give or take a degree or two. When you reach the point of heat exhaustion, your core, where your vital organs reside, has heated to 102°F (39°C) or more.

When you develop heat exhaustion, the mechanisms your body uses to regulate your internal temperature go haywire. At this point, your body has lost the ability to cool itself, and your internal temperature will only get hotter unless you take steps to cool off externally. Your whole body needs time to cool because when your temperature gets to 103°F (39°C), you're getting very close to the shutdown levels of heatstroke, which can be fatal.

A heatstroke takes time to develop, and it is always preceded by heat exhaustion. Take the signs of heat exhaustion seriously and treat them immediately. It is your best chance to prevent heatstroke.

Symptoms of Heat Exhaustion

The symptoms of heat exhaustion are any or all of the following:

- a sudden, massive increase in sweating

- a sudden decrease in sweating

- muscle cramps

- extreme weakness

- dizziness

- headache

- nausea or vomiting

- fainting

Signs of Heat Exhaustion

Signs of heat exhaustion are any or all of the following:

- pale skin color

- goose bumps and skin that has become inappropriately cool to the touch

- a weak pulse

- low blood pressure

- confusion*

* It is this risk of confusion that makes it very important that you work with a partner to treat symptoms so you can monitor each other.

How to Treat Heat Exhaustion

- Stop activity immediately. Not when you get to a finishing place, not in a few minutes. Immediately. Your body generates heat with activity, and if you don't stop, you will get heatstroke.

- Find the coolest spot available and lie down.

- Drink water or a sports drink. When you reach the point of heat exhaustion, you're almost always dehydrated. The fluids will help cool you and also help your circulation work more efficiently to cool you off.

- Stay cool the rest of the day.

- Don't drink caffeine. It's a diuretic and can adversely affect your circulation.

- Don't drink high-sugar drinks. They are more difficult to absorb.

In a spectrum of heat-related illnesses, first comes heat exhaustion. If you heed its warnings and do the right things, you can prevent what's sure to follow otherwise—potentially deadly heatstroke.

HEATSTROKE

During heatstroke, your heat-regulating system malfunctions. It's like your body has given up (or burned out). Your vital organs shut down. One of the first organs that shows damage is the brain. Therefore, many of the warning signs and symptoms of heatstroke are related to brain function.

Signs and Symptoms of Heatstroke

Remember, heat exhaustion always precedes heatstroke. In addition to the signs and symptoms of heat exhaustion, warning signs of heatstroke are any or all of the following:

- agitation

- confusion

- hallucinations

- disorientation

- euphoria

- seizure

- coma

How to Treat Heatstroke

Call 911 immediately. The victim needs medical assistance and will not get better on his own. His organs are cooking. Until help arrives, cool the person off as best you can by doing the following:

- Move the victim into air-conditioning, if available. Otherwise, have the victim lie down in the shade.

- If the person is unconscious, place him on his side so his tongue won't impede his airway (see page 43).

- Take off all but the victim's underclothes.

- Spray or bathe the victim with cool/cold water.

- Soak a sheet in the coolest water possible and wrap it around the victim's bare skin.

- If you have ice, place a pack on the person's groin and armpits, and under his neck.

- Fan the person for the cooling effect of evaporation.

- If you have access to and training for IV fluids, now's the time to give them.

There is a debate about whether someone with heatstroke should soak in a tub of ice water if it's available. The problem is, if the person's heart stops, it's difficult to do CPR in the tub. I think you should do whatever cools the victim in the quickest way and with the least effort on the victim's part.

Even if you fully hydrate and cool a heatstroke victim, he will have multiple-organ damage. Get him to a medical facility as soon as possible.

HYPOTHERMIA

The official definition of hypothermia is body temperature below 95°F (35°C). By the time you're that cold, you're probably shivering pretty hard, and that actually works well to warm you up. Shivering increases your metabolism, which causes your cells to produce more heat. But if you don't get out of the cold, your body tires out and the shivering stops. After that, you're headed for major trouble because you've lost one of your body's last efforts to keep itself warm.

Prevention Tip: The air temperature doesn't have to be freezing for a person to experience hypothermia. It only needs to be cold enough to lower the person's body temperature a few degrees. Usually that takes an air temperature of less than 50°F (10°C), but not always.

Factors that Increase the Risk of Hypothermia

The following make you more susceptible to the cold and therefore at higher risk for hypothermia at higher temperatures:

1. **Getting wet.** When you are wet, you get cold a lot quicker, and at higher temperatures, than when you are dry. Wet clothes conduct heat about five times more rapidly than air. When you are immersed in water, you conduct heat 25 times faster than when you are surrounded by air. Your body temperature can get dangerously low in any water below about 91°F (33°C). Of course, the colder the water, the faster your body temperature drops. Hypothermia-related deaths occur annually in boating accidents and the like, which explains most of the hypothermia deaths in Florida and Hawaii.

2. **Taking alcohol or drugs.** They dull your senses (especially if you pass out, to point out the obvious), so you don't realize you're cold until it's too late. Alcohol also dilates (increases the size of) surface veins, so your blood flows closer to the surface of your skin, releasing body heat that is normally kept in your core for your vital organs.

3. **Being a victim of trauma.** Trauma can wreak havoc with body-temperature regulators. Also the victim might not notice how cold she is getting due to pain or an impaired mental status. If you're treating a trauma victim, remember to cover the victim with a blanket or whatever is available. Also get the person out of wet clothes.

4. **Age.** As you age, your temperature regulators don't work as well. The decline can begin even as young as age 65. Children under age three have more skin surface versus body mass. Heat escapes through the skin, so they lose heat faster. In addition, the cold has a tendency to sneak up in on both these age groups before anyone notices.

5. **Having a chronic disease.** Hypothyroidism, Parkinson's, heart disease and severe infections are examples of the many problems that

affect your body's heat regulation. People with these issues can't fight off the cold as well as people without health issues.

Ways to Prevent Hypothermia

- **Dress in layers**. Keep warm, but avoid getting so hot that you start sweating.

- **Stay dry.** If you get wet, change clothes. If you can't change clothes, try to at least wrap something around you that's waterproof to cut down on moisture evaporation, which takes away more heat.

- **Stay out of the wind.**

- **Stay hydrated.** Drink warm, noncaffeinated drinks if available.

- **Eat regularly.** Calories are how your body generates heat.

- **Avoid sleeping on the ground.** The bare ground will quickly suck away your body heat. Even the bottom of your tent and your sleeping bag may not be enough to protect you from losing heat to the cold ground overnight. Use a sleeping pad designed for camping or, if one isn't available, create a debris nest—a very thick pile of dry leaves, pine needles and other ground covering that traps dead air between your body and the ground. A flattened cardboard box is an excellent bottom for a debris nest.

HOW TO TREAT HYPOTHERMIA

The effects of hypothermia are progressive. The signs and symptoms may come on earlier or later, or may overlap in different people. For example, it can be impossible to know if a confused person is in mild or moderate hypothermia. Because hypothermia can cause confusion and lapses in judgment, it's important to work with a partner so you can monitor each other.

The stages below are only to give you some very general guidelines. For treatment purposes, it's always best to err on the cautious side.

Warning Signs of Mild Hypothermia

- shivering

- trouble talking

- confusion

- deteriorating judgment

- amnesia (forgetfulness)

- increased heart rate

How to Treat Mild Hypothermia

With mild hypothermia, your body is still generating heat, so don't let it escape.

- Take shelter, in a heated location if possible. At the least, get behind a wind block and start a fire if possible.

- Get out of any wet clothes or cover yourself in something waterproof.

- Cover your whole body, including your head, hands, neck and face to trap in body heat.

- Stay off the cold ground. Use a sleeping pad or build a debris nest.

- Drink noncaffeinated fluids (warm if possible).

- Eat a snack to give your body the fuel it needs to generate heat.

- Don't rub your skin to warm up. Vigorous rubbing dilates those surface vessels the same way alcohol does. It makes you feel warm at the expense of taking heat from your vital organs.

Warning Signs of Moderate Hypothermia

- stops shivering (shivering is a major defense against the cold)

- increased confusion

- paradoxical undressing (taking off clothes; no one's sure exactly why this happens)

- slowing heart rate that may become irregular

At this stage, the least bit of bumping or agitation can set off lethal heart rhythms in the victim. Even at rest, the person is at high risk.

How to Treat Moderate Hypothermia

1. Continue treatment for mild hypothermia.

2. Place heating pads, hot packs, hot water bottles, etc. under the arms. Protect the skin from burns by using light-weight clothes or mittens between the external heat and the skin.

3. Be gentle when treating someone else. At a cold body temperature, your heart becomes very sensitive to jostling and tends to go into bad rhythms.

4. If the person is confused, keep an eye on him. Calm him by talking, and ask if he has any medical problems. Low blood sugar or a fall could be causing or contributing to the confusion.

5. A last resort is sharing body heat. If you're getting really, really cold, and there's no other way, two or three people can get under blankets, take off their clothes and get skin to skin. It's worth a try.

Warning Signs of Severe Hypothermia

- coma

- fatal heart rhythm (ventricular fibrillation), meaning there is no pulse and the person is in cardiac arrest

How to Treat Severe Hypothermia

One of the keys to treating an unconscious person with hypothermia is to get the person someplace that has advanced warming techniques like warmed IV fluids, warmed breathing devices and just plain heat. A severely hypothermic person has lost much of her ability to generate body heat.

Do what you can to get the person transferred, but keep yourself safe. If you're out in the middle of a frozen nowhere, there is a finite amount of time and energy you can expend before you put yourself in danger of exhaustion and severe hypothermia.

Here are some things you can do to help someone with severe hypothermia until you can get him to a treatment facility. But remember, everything must be done gently. A cold heart is easily irritated. A little jostling can change a normal heartbeat rhythm into a lethal one.

Short-term treatment when professional medical help is less than two hours away

1. Unless you know there has been no head or neck trauma, stabilize the neck before moving (see page 165).

2. Check for breathing. Severe hypothermia is one of the only instances when nonmedical people should consider mouth-to-mouth respirations (see page 42).

   - If there's no breathing, run a finger around the inside of the mouth to make sure there's nothing blocking the airway. If there is, remove it and recheck for breathing.

- If you're sure head or neck trauma was not involved, grab both sides of the face and tilt the head backward. This should also open the mouth. Recheck for breathing.

- If you can't rule out head or neck trauma, kneel at the top of the victim's head, keeping the head still with your hands. Place your thumbs behind each side of the jaw below the ears and push the lower jaw outward. Recheck for breathing.

- If there's still no breathing or if the respirations are six per minute or less, start mouth-to-mouth respirations.

- If you have a commercial barrier (CPR mask) use it to avoid coming in contact with the victim's fluids. If not, consider putting a large hole in any waterproof covering (exam gloves, plastic bag) and placing it between your mouth and hers.

- Kneel over the victim, pinch her nose shut, seal your mouth over hers and blow a puff of air just strong enough to make her chest rise. If it doesn't rise, recheck the mouth and reposition the head or jaw.

- Repeat the breaths about every five seconds (12 breaths per minute).

3. Check the pulse. Check well. The blood vessels close to the skin constrict when a person is cold, and the pulse rate slows down, making a pulse harder to detect. If the person is breathing, her heart is probably beating. Be very cautious; if there is a heartbeat, chest compressions or any movement will likely cause the heart (which is very irritable in hypothermia) to go into cardiac arrest.

4. If you're as certain as you can be that the heart is not beating and expert help or transfer is possible within two hours, you may begin chest compressions (see page 39). But your priorities need to be ventilations and getting the person to expert help as gently as possible.

5. Chest compressions or not, if you think there's a chance for expert help or transfer within two hours, don't warm the person. There is a phenomenon known as the "metabolic icebox effect" in which, in rare instances, the body's metabolism slows down so far in the cold that its organs can stay alive for several hours without serious damage. The person is better off in this state until transferred to a facility with sophisticated equipment.

Long-term treatment when professional medical help is not coming
If you expect help within a couple of hours, the above may be all you need to do. If it's going to be longer, or not coming, consider the following:

1. Get the person to a warm, safe place. This is the person's only chance of survival. If shelter is available, and you're the only person who can help, it's better to concentrate on transfer and forget about chest compressions until the former is complete. If shelter is not available, at least get the victim out of the wind by moving behind or setting up some kind of wind block. After you are in the shelter, get the person near an external heat source. Any kind will do—from a fire to a space heater to a car heater—as long as it doesn't damage the skin.

2. If there's a second person to help, check the pulse and breathing again. Start chest compressions, if needed, and have the other person do steps three and four. If you're the only one there, do steps three and four before beginning chest compressions.

3. Cover the victim from head to toe, removing any wet clothes first. A sleeping bag is ideal, and some waterproof material (even garbage bags) to go outside the other covers is even better, but even dry newspapers can be good makeshift insulation. Leave an opening for breathing.

4. Keep the victim off the cold ground as much as possible. Use a sleep pad or, if nothing else, pile up a bunch of debris (nothing sharp or wet) for the person to lie down on.

5. If available, add hot packs to the neck and groin and under the arms. Cover the packs with cloth or mittens to protect the skin from burns.

6. If someone can start an IV, heat the IV fluids to at least body temperature and no warmer than, say, a hot bath.

Treatment Tip: Health-care providers who treat people with hypothermia have a saying: "They're not dead until they're warm and dead." Miraculous recoveries do occur, and rarely, people survive longer when they have a low body temperature than they would otherwise. But each instance is unique. Don't endanger yourself from the cold or fatigue. There's another saying: "Sometimes, no matter what you do, people die." If you focus your early efforts on preventing hypothermia, your odds of survival will greatly increase. Know the risks and avoid them.

FROSTBITE

Frostbite happens when any part of your skin, or the tissue underneath, freezes. Freezing causes tissue damage. There's no way around it. So your first priority should be prevention. If frostbite occurs, your goal is to limit the damage.

Frostnip is when your skin is just starting to freeze. The skin becomes numb and frosted in appearance. If you can catch it and warm the skin at this stage, there may be no permanent damage.

Ways to Prevent Frostbite

1. Keep all of your skin covered in freezing weather.

2. Stay out of the wind, which greatly increases your risk. The more wind exposure there is, the higher the outside temperature can be to still cause frostbite. If you're skiing or snowmobiling, even running, remember to cover up with layers.

3. Know the early signs of numbness, tingling or pain of the affected skin and start acting before it's too late. Frostnip occurs just before frostbite. If your skin is numb or looks frosted, take action.

Warning Signs of Frostbite

- numbness of the affected skin

- tingling or pain

- white, grayish or bluish skin

- hard skin or skin that indents with pressing

HOW TO TREAT FROSTBITE

If the frostbite is accompanied by hypothermia, treat the hypothermia first (see page 77).

If tissue is frozen, don't rewarm it until you know you can keep it from refreezing—even if this means you have to walk on frostbitten feet. Walking on frozen feet can definitely cause damage, but allowing the tissue to thaw and then refreeze can cause much more damage.

1. Rewarm the tissue.

The best first aid method for rewarming frostbite is to immerse the area in warm water (100°F to 108°F [38°C to 42°C]). The tissue should thaw within 15 to 30 minutes. If you don't have a thermometer, gauge the temperature with your hand. Make it as hot as possible, but stop before it is too uncomfortable to leave your hand in it.

During and after rewarming, keep the following in mind:

- Be very gentle with the damaged tissue. Handle it with care.

- Don't walk, stand or put pressure on the injured area.

- Let the injured area air dry. Don't towel dry or rub.

Rewarming Tips

- Keep the water moving a little. It helps keep the warmest water next to the injury.

- Don't let the water get too hot or too cold. Keep the temperature constant, or more skin damage may occur.

- Expect swelling, large blisters and severe pain. Those are signs the tissue is rewarming. Don't remove blisters, even the large ones, unless they're already leaking. A sealed blister is a sterile environment and limits infection risk. Take aspirin or ibuprofen (Advil or Motrin) for pain, if available, because they provide additional frostbite benefits that aid in healing.

2. Limit swelling.

When frostbite injures tissue, it can cause significant swelling. Keep the injured area at heart level or above by reclining your body and elevating the injured area. Don't use restrictive dressings.

To keep the blood circulating and aid healing:

- Consider taking a vasodilator (medicine that opens up the blood vessel flow). Some blood pressure medicines help if you're already on them. Aspirin may help. Niacin is worth a try if you don't have ulcers. (Niacin may make your overall skin flush and tingle.)

- Don't smoke. Smoking constricts blood vessels.

3. Dress the frostbitten area.

- Keep absorbent padding, such as gauze or cotton, between injured fingers or toes.

- Use antibacterial cream. Silvadene (1 percent silver sulfadiazine) is a good one. Triple antibiotic, gentamycin and bacitracin are alternatives.

- Cover the wound with a light dressing or leave it open to the air.

- Start antibiotics, if available (see page 31).

4. Prevent complications.

Complications from frostbite include cutoff of circulation, infection and pain. To best avoid these complications, get expert medical help as soon as you can.

- **To prevent cutoff of circulation:** Keep the area elevated and avoid any constrictive clothing, jewelry or dressing.

- **To prevent infection:** Keep the area clean and dressed. Use antibiotics such as cephalexin, erythromycin, amoxicillin-clavulanate or ciprofloxacin, if available.

- **To manage pain:** The victim may experience waves of pain that come and go. Continue whatever pain medication you have as needed.

Some of the tissue may turn black. This is dead skin. As with the blisters, don't attempt to remove it. It will naturally slough off in several weeks. In the meantime, you need to keep the area clean and dressed.

FIVE

SKIN WOUNDS

Wound treatment is a big part of first aid. Infection is a potential serious complication of any wound, no matter how big or small it is. This chapter deals with cuts and lacerations, gunshot wounds and burns.

MAKESHIFT WOUND-TREATMENT TOOLS

How to Make a Sterile Dressing

Normally, you can use sterile gauze to dress or pack a wound. But if no sterile gauze is available, find any clean rags or cloths and sterilize them. You can do this in one of two ways:

- Boil them in water for one to three minutes. (Cool before packing them into the wound.)

- Soak the clean rags with a mixture of nine parts clean water to one part Betadine (povidone-iodine). For instance, mix 9 ounces (270ml) of water with 1 ounce (30ml) of 10 percent Betadine.

After you sterilize the dressing material, apply antibiotic ointment to the wound (or to the material if you're using the gauze for packing). Then cover the wound with the rags. Tape the rags or tie a cloth around them to keep the dressing in place. (Important: Don't tie tightly enough to cut off circulation.)

Change the dressing daily or at least every two days. Also change it if the dressing gets wet or especially dirty.

If you can't sterilize the cloths, just coat the wound with antibacterial ointment or honey (see page 33) and cover with a clean cloth.

How to Make a Pressure Dressing

Pressure dressings are bandages that press down on a wound. Most of the time, this is to stop the bleeding.

Never use a pressure dressing for a full wrap: Don't wrap a pressure dressing all the way around an extremity (arm or leg) if you can help it. If you wrap any bandage too tight around an extremity, you've got a tourniquet. The bandage will also become a tourniquet if the extremity swells and the bandage has no give. You've cut off blood supply coming from the arteries, and the tissue distal to the dressing (the side farthest from the heart) is going to die.

Use bulk to add pressure: To your normal dressing, add extra layers of gauze or bunch up some clean cloth on the wound area. Sanitary napkins are another option. When you tape the dressing down, the bulk of the extra dressing will press on the wound, but it will also have some give so it doesn't cut off circulation if the area swells.

Tape the dressing down firmly, placing tape only about one-half or two-thirds of the way around an extremity. Or use an elastic bandage instead of tape. Wrap the bandage firm but not too tight. You should be able to stick a couple of fingers under the wrap.

If the hand or foot gets discolored, cold or tingly, loosen the pressure dressing immediately. Until you can readjust it, you can press on the bandage with your hand to stop the bleeding.

HOW TO STERILIZE INSTRUMENTS

Unless you have a commercial autoclave and a power source, or some prepackaged sterile products, you're going to have to make do with what you have and sterilize as best you can.

Before you sterilize, always clean any obvious debris off your instruments. Clean with soap and water or alcohol. Use a cloth or brush if needed.

Quick Methods for Sterilization

- **Heating the instrument.** Hold the part that's going to touch the injury over an open flame. If the handle is also metal, find something to hold the instrument with so you don't burn your fingers. Heat until the metal turns red; that's long enough. Then let the instrument cool, and you're ready. If I have alcohol, I also like to dip the instrument in that just for good measure.

- **Using a disinfectant.** If you don't have fire and you're in a hurry, you can wipe the instrument off with a clean cloth soaked in iodine, povidone-iodine (Betadine) or alcohol. No clean cloth? Dip the instrument in the solution and stir it around for ten seconds.

Sterilization Methods that Take Longer

- **Boiling.** This is a good method for larger instruments or those that might melt under the flame. Let the instrument soak in boiling water for 20 minutes.

- **Use a disinfectant for a longer amount of time.** Soaking the instrument in disinfectant for 20 minutes is better than the wiping/dipping method.

WHAT TO DO BEFORE AND AFTER A PROCEDURE

1. Always wash your hands.

2. Wear clean gloves, if available, to protect yourself and the victim.

3. Wash any object that came in contact with infectious bodily fluids with disinfectants immediately after the procedure is finished.

CUTS AND LACERATIONS

A laceration is when soft tissue on the body is torn, cut or punctured. Some small cuts bleed profusely, and other more serious cuts hardly bleed at all. There are deep cuts, shallow nicks, scrapes and gashes on the face or the foot. To know which ones are "serious" can often be a judgment call. But even the tiniest wound is potentially serious because it damages our first defense against germs—the physical barrier of our skin. If not cleaned and kept that way, that little ant bite could lead to a mighty infection.

There are six steps to treating any cut or laceration:

1. Stop the bleeding.

2. Assess the damage.

3. Clean the wound.

4. Decide on treatment.

5. Close the wound (if appropriate).

6. Watch for infection.

Treatment Tip: Protect yourself before you treat someone else's wound. If there's a chance you could be exposed to blood, wear vinyl or latex gloves, or some sort of plastic cover for your hands, and also wear protective eyewear if available.

Blood loss is the most immediate threat to life presented by a cut or laceration. Simply put, the longer, faster or more volume you bleed, the more dangerous and life-threatening the wound becomes. Your first step is always to stop the bleeding, or at least reduce the amount of bleeding as much as you can.

Memorize this: First, stop the bleeding. Try direct pressure first.

STEP 1: STOP THE BLEEDING

Applying direct pressure stops the vast majority of bleeding from wounds. Press a clean cloth or gauze against the wound. Usually it doesn't take a lot of pressure, just enough to push the injured blood vessels shut. If you don't have cloth or gauze, apply direct pressure with your free hand (clean your hand as much as possible first; use gloves or some other protection if you are treating someone else). Most bleeding stops with this method by clotting in five to ten minutes, but sometimes it can take as much as 30 minutes.

Direct pressure works because it keeps the blood in place within the wound, giving the clotting material your blood naturally produces time to bind together to close the wound (in other words, start forming a scab).

SKIN WOUNDS

Special Circumstances

- If the wound is on an extremity (arm or leg), raise the area of injury to heart level or above to decrease the blood flow. Continue to apply pressure.

- If you're treating a cut finger, squeeze around the wound with your other hand. Also take off rings right away. You'll be glad you did if the finger swells.

- For a larger wound area, push down on the entire bleeding area with your palm (using gauze or cloth if available).

- For gaping wounds with a lot of bleeding, try packing the wound with a bunch of clean cloths or gauze and applying pressure.

- If there's a broken bone nearby or underneath the wound, try to press carefully enough that you don't move the bone. But your primary concern is to stop any serious bleeding by any means possible.

When the Bleeding Won't Stop If You Let Go of the Pressure

If the bleeding stops with pressure but starts back up when you release, even after holding for five to 30 minutes, apply a pressure dressing (see page 89). The bleeding may restart because of one of the following reasons:

1. The person may have a bleeding disorder, or

2. The person may have ingested food or medicine (even days before) that can affect clotting time. Some examples are:

   - blood thinners, such as Plavix or Coumadin

   - aspirin

   - any nonsteroidal anti-inflammatory drugs (NSAIDs), such as ibuprofen, naproxen and others, which can prolong bleeding a bit but not as much as aspirin

   - certain herbs, such as garlic, ginger, ginkgo, and feverfew

   - fish oil

   - vitamin E

What to Do When Pressure Won't Stop the Bleeding

When to give up on direct pressure depends on how much bleeding there is. For a gushing artery, you may start these steps within seconds. For a slow ooze, you might wait as long as 30 minutes. If pressure is not stopping the bleeding, here are three other options that may stop the bleeding:

- Use a commercial quick-clotting material such as QuikClot or Celox. It comes in granules or adhered to a cloth. The cloth type is much less messy and easy to get out of the wound when the time comes. Wipe away excess blood before using and follow the label's instructions. The problem with using this material is it's so easy, it's often used for any wound. Sooner or later the material has to be removed and the bleeding may start again. Be sure to save this method for bleeding that won't stop with direct pressure.

- If the cut is associated with a broken bone that's out of place, traction (steadily pulling on the bone without jerking, see page 177) to get it in place might stop the bleeding.

- Apply a tourniquet (see page 96).

STEP 2: ASSESS THE DAMAGE
Potential Life-threatening Wounds

When you're dealing with a serious wound, sometimes there's just not much you can do in the field. Your best option is to get treatment at a medical facility, even if you're in a remote location and it might be very hard—even a bit dangerous—to get there. If a wound presents any of these situations, you need treatment at a medical facility:

- The bleeding won't stop with direct pressure or commercial clotting material, or you require a tourniquet. (Getting professional medical help fairly quickly could save a life or limb.)

- Fingers or toes are becoming cold or discolored. That's a sign that an essential artery may have been damaged. If the artery is not surgically reconnected within hours, the tissue supplied by that artery will die and become gangrenous. After that, the dead tissue needs a surgical amputation, or it's sure to get an infection that will spread into the healthy flesh and the bloodstream. You can get very sick and even die.

- The chest cavity or abdominal cavity has been punctured. These wounds present the risk of unseen bleeding, and they are extremely likely to develop serious infections.

- It's a neck wound that involves the airway. Apply cold packs for swelling, if available.

HOW TO APPLY A TOURNIQUET

If nothing else is helping and blood is spurting rapidly out of an extremity wound, you may have to resort to a tourniquet to save a life. If you don't have a ready-made tourniquet, use some sturdy material, such as a belt or a rolled-up shirt, that is 1 to 2 inches (3 to 5cm) wide.

One way to make a tourniquet is to tear a thick strip of cloth and tie both ends to a single stick or anything firm. Apply the tourniquet above the wound, and twist the stick to tighten the cloth until the bleeding stops.

- Wrap the tourniquet around the extremity. Place it a few inches (centimeters) above the wound because a cut artery may spasm and shorten a couple of inches (centimeters).

- Tighten the tourniquet until the bleeding stops. (If you need more pressure than you can apply, tie the tourniquet ends to a sturdy rod or stick. Wind the stick.)

- If you plan on getting expert help within two hours, keep the tourniquet tight.

- If help is more than two hours away, after that time loosen the tourniquet a bit so blood flow isn't entirely cut off to the area below the wound. If you can loosen the tourniquet a bit and stop the bleeding with pressure, you have a better chance of saving the limb.

Warning: Using a tourniquet can cause permanent damage to the part of the limb not getting the blood supply. In fact, you could end up losing the entire limb. However, sometimes that's the sacrifice a person has to make to save a life.

Wounds that Can Cause Permanent Damage

A wound that may not be immediately life-threatening can still have common and serious complications that may cause long-term or permanent damage without proper treatment. The following types of wounds need treatment at a medical facility, but you have longer to try to obtain it:

- **Open fracture** (also called a compound fracture). If a broken bone is associated with the cut, the wound is at a very high risk for a serious infection. The wound needs to be thoroughly and surgically cleaned out in as sterile a setting as possible. Try to get expert help within 18 hours. Your risk of infection increases the longer you wait.

- **Nerve damage.** Is the area distal to the wound (the side away from the heart) numb? You may have severed a nerve. You usually have a few days to see a surgeon before the damage becomes irreparable.

- **Tendon damage.** Have you lost movement? If so, you may have cut a tendon. Again, this is not an emergency, but an expert needs to see it within a few days for repair.

STEP 3: CLEAN THE WOUND

Cleaning a wound is a three-step process:

1. If there's any noticeable debris, try to pick it out. Tweezers can help. (See page 108 for more on removing foreign objects from wounds.)

2. Use soap and water for superficial cuts and a cotton swab for hard-to-reach areas within the wound.

3. Irrigate.

Types of Irrigating Solution

- Wash out wounds with water clean enough for drinking. If you only

HOW TO INSPECT OR CLEAN A BLEEDING WOUND

Temporarily stop the bleeding by applying pressure on both sides of the wound. If you need a free hand, try releasing pressure on one side, then the other to see where most of the bleeding is coming from.

Arteries pump blood from the heart, and veins drain blood back to it. If the blood is oozing out rather than spurting, it is usually from a vein. Try applying pressure to the area away from your heart (the side closer to the foot or hand). If the blood is spurting, it's coming from an artery. Try applying pressure on the side of the wound nearest the heart.

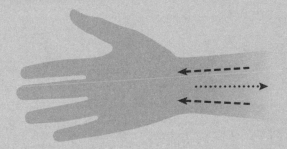

Arteries (represented by dashed lines) carry blood away from the heart. Veins (represented by dotted line) carry blood toward the heart.

have access to contaminated water, see page 54 for ways to kill the bad germs before using.

- Strong solutions such as undiluted peroxide or iodine have a tendency to damage tissue a bit. But if that's all you've got, use it.

Amount of Irrigating Solution

- If available, use a minimum of 2 ounces (60ml) of water per ½ inch (13mm) of wound. Shallower wounds may require less water, deeper ones more.

- Use 20 ounces (600ml) of water per ½ inch (13mm) of wound to irrigate wounds associated with broken bones. Even the smallest amount of bacteria can cause big problems if it gets in the bone. (Bone doesn't have the same defenses that soft tissue has to fight off bacteria.)

How to Irrigate

Pressure cleaning usually does the best job. (Soaking doesn't help much, and scrubbing can damage tissue—although sometimes it has to be done.) To pressure clean, just stick your cut under a running faucet.

If you don't have access to running water, here are three ways to create your own pressure:

1. Fill a water jug or plastic bag with water and poke a small hole in the bottom. Squeeze the jug and direct the water to the wound.

2. Fill a bulb syringe (a rubber, teardrop-shaped squirter commonly used on babies) with water and squirt it in the cut.

3. Fill a large syringe with water. Remove any needle and squirt the water into the wound.

STEP 4: DECIDE ON TREATMENT

You have about ten to 12 hours to decide whether or not to close the wound. The risk of getting a serious infection such as an abscess (trapped bacteria and pus) increases dramatically if you close a wound after that amount of time.

Of course, not all wounds need to be closed. Any wound that is a nick, not deep, not over a joint, or shorter than about ¼ inch (6mm) will heal fine on its own as long as you keep it clean and covered.

You should not attempt to close some deeper and larger wounds on your own because of the risk of infection.

Reasons to NOT Close a Wound:

- You can get expert help within ten to 12 hours.

- It's a puncture wound (much deeper than it is wide; these are difficult to clean adequately).

- It's a mouth or tongue cut (see page 107).

- It's dirty and you can't clean it well.

- It's large and deep. (It will be very hard to clean completely.)

- It involves a broken bone.

- It's a bite (all that bacteria).

Closing most of these wounds would mean closing up the bacteria as well—trapping it in a warm, moist, nutritious place to thrive and grow. In a closed wound, the bacteria is completely protected from outside interference. This can result in a serious infection. If you leave the wound open, you can continue to clean it.

How to Treat Wounds You Don't Close

Until you can get help, do your best to keep a wound you don't close infection-free by doing the following:

- Clean it as best you can (irrigation).

- Pack with sterile, wet gauze. (Use drinkable water to wet the gauze.) If you don't have sterile gauze, see page 89 for how to make a makeshift dressing. Packing the wound keeps it from bleeding or closing up too soon. (You want it healing from the inside first.) It also keeps the healing inner tissues moist.

- Cover the wound in antibacterial ointment or honey (see page 33). Put a clean—preferably sterile—dry cloth or gauze on top and tape it in place.

- Remove the packed materials and repack with fresh ones once or twice a day.

Many of these wounds can still be closed by a medical professional within a few days of injury if you're able to get medical help right away.

Treatment Tip: Super glue is great for tiny cuts or cracks on your fingers or shallow wounds ¼ inch (6mm) in length or less. After you thoroughly clean the cut (irrigate), pinch the area together and apply the glue.

STEP 5: CLOSE THE WOUND

If you've gone through step four and decide you need to close the wound, you have several options: sutures (stitches), staples, glue or tape, or hair and string (for a head wound).

Sewing with sutures takes hands-on training to learn, so it will not be covered in this book. Use that option only if you have proper training. The other three options are explained in this section.

Whichever method you choose for closing the wound, apply a dressing afterward (see page 89).

How to Staple a Wound Closed

Stapling a wound requires a special kind of staple gun made specifically for stapling skin. You will also need a special staple remover specifically made to remove skin staples.

To staple a wound closed:

1. Thoroughly clean the wound (see page 98).

2. Close the cut edges of the wound with a free hand. Have the edges touching but not overlapping.

3. Press firmly and use the staple gun as if you're stapling paper to a wall.

How to Glue or Tape a Wound Closed

I like this method. It's easy and you're more likely to have the materials on hand. You'll need Steri-Strips (skinny, sterile tape), butterfly bandages or regular tape (duct tape is great). Glue would also be helpful. If you're using regular tape, tear strips about ½ inch (13mm) wide and about 2 to 3 inches (5 to 8mm) long.

1. After thoroughly cleaning the wound, use a clean cloth to dry the skin around the cut.

2. You can help the tape stick better by applying a little super glue to the skin immediately adjacent to both sides of the wound.

3. Place the tape perpendicular (at a right angle) across the wound. Start at one end of the wound and stick half of the tape on one side of the skin next to the wound.

4. Bring the cut edges together using your hand, and press the tape down on the other side of the wound.

5. Continue holding the wound together. Take the next strip of tape and stick it down, leaving about a ¼-inch (6mm) space between the pieces (so the wound can drain if it needs to).

6. Continue placing tape perpendicularly down the length of the wound until it is closed.

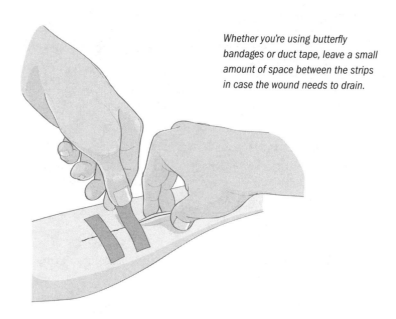

Whether you're using butterfly bandages or duct tape, leave a small amount of space between the strips in case the wound needs to drain.

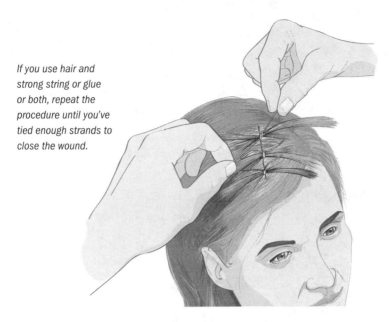

If you use hair and strong string or glue or both, repeat the procedure until you've tied enough strands to close the wound.

How to Use Hair and String to Close Head Wounds

If you have a head wound and aren't bald, tape isn't going to stick to your scalp. You might try super gluing a small wound closed, but another alternative is to use your hair to your advantage.

For this method to work, your hair needs to be at least 1 inch (3cm) long. You'll also need strong string (such as dental floss) cut into pieces that are about 2 inches (5cm) long. Super glue is helpful and, if necessary, can even substitute for the string.

1. Place a piece of the string lengthwise on top of the wound.

2. Starting at the top edge of the wound, use both hands to grab a section of hair on each side of the wound.

3. Twist the sections of hair on each side separately so you have two rope-like strands of hair—one on each side.

4. Cross the two twisted sections over the wound to pull the wound closed, but make sure the string isn't closed in the wound.

5. Pick up the string beneath the crossed hair and tie it around the hair to hold the hair in place. You can add some glue to the string if you want—or just glue the strands in place if you have no string.

6. Work your way down the length of the wound in sections, repeating steps one through four until the wound is closed.

STEP 6: WATCH FOR INFECTION

Infections are a common complication with cuts and lacerations.

Warning Signs of Skin Infection

- an increase in warmth or redness around the wound

- a red, swollen spot on the skin

- red streaks running toward the heart (a sign the infection is draining into the lymph system)

- pus

- fever

HOW TO TREAT A SKIN INFECTION

Use a moderate amount of heat on the area—never hot enough to burn the skin. Soak a cloth in warm water, and apply to the infected area as much as possible—a minimum of 20 minutes at a time, four times a day. Many times this will resolve small areas of infection. Otherwise the infected area could improve in one of two ways:

1. The body will fight the infection, and it will just fade away.

2. The infected area may start draining pus through the stitches, staples or tape. If the drainage is more than a little—enough to, say, soak your dressing—remove the stitches, staples or tape and reopen the wound. Then treat it as if you'd never closed it in the first place. Irrigate it until it is clean, and pack with sterile, wet gauze.

Serious infection: If the redness radiates more than ½ inch (13mm) around the edges of the wound, you have a fever or pus, or red streaks are running toward your heart, the infection is getting serious and you need oral antibiotics (see page 31). If they're not available, continue the above treatment until you can get some.

CUTS IN THE MOUTH OR TONGUE

Don't stitch the inner lips, inner cheeks, tongue or gums unless the wound is big and gaping or won't stop bleeding. There's no way to keep a mouth wound dry or bacteria-free. Bacteria can attach to the stitches and make any infection worse. Also, infected wounds need to be able to drain if bacteria and pus build up. Otherwise, all that stuff might get trapped, and you'd have an abscess (trapped bacteria and pus).

How to Treat a Cut Inside Your Mouth

1. **Clean the cut.** Pick out any obvious debris. Irrigate the cut by swishing water in your mouth or squirting water into the cut with a bulb syringe or regular syringe with the needle removed.

2. **Stop the bleeding.** Stuff a clean cloth between the cut and your gum or teeth. (No cloth? Squeeze, pinch—apply pressure of some sort.) Ten minutes of direct pressure should do it—20 at the most.

3. **Ice the cut for five to ten minutes, if possible.** You can use the ice as part of the compression inside the mouth to stop the bleeding, or wrap cloth around the ice and use it on the outside.

4. **Start an oral antibiotic,** if available. You can expect any mouth cut to get swollen, painful and infected. The mouth is full of bacteria. There's no way to keep the wound sterile. (See page 30 to learn more about getting antibiotics.)

5. **Eat soft food** to avoid further abrasions, cuts and irritation. Don't chew on that side. Avoid salty foods (they make the cut sting).

If the cut extends through to the outside of the cheeks, chin, or lips, clean the outside, and close the exterior wound like you would any other cut. (But keep the inner mouth or tongue wound open.)

If the outside, colored part of the lip is lacerated, that's more of a problem. You want it to grow back straight, so a doctor should see deep cuts to the lip ASAP. If that's not possible, tape it back as straight as you can, keeping the colored edge as even as you can.

REMOVING SMALL FOREIGN OBJECTS IN THE SKIN

When something penetrates the skin and becomes embedded, two bad things can happen:

1. The object can damage nerves, tendons or blood vessels.

2. If the area around the object gets infected, it's likely to stay that way until the object is taken out.

If You Can See the Object

Wait a few seconds before you pull it out. Think: How deep did it go? Do you think you can get it all out? Make sure you can get a good grip on it. If it falls apart easily, like rotten wood, and some breaks off in the wound, you're really worse off than when you started.

If You Can't Grip It But Can See It

You'll need some sterile tweezers and maybe a sterile needle. (See page 90 for how to sterilize instruments.) Use the needle to pick at the skin surface to remove the object or to better see it for removal with tweezers.

If You Can't See or Feel the Foreign Object

Leave it alone. Digging around for it is like trying to find a needle in a haystack. Treat with moist heat like you would for infections (see page 106). Often, small pieces of metal just settle in and cause no harm. For most other materials, your body wants it out as much as you do and will use its immune responses to try to bring the object to the skin's surface. If the object isn't too deep, it may just pop out in a few days. Small slivers of glass often do this. Alternately, it may come to a head with a soft bulging in the skin. At that point you could prick the bulging area with a sterile needle or knife, and often the object will spit right out.

Treatment Tip: Never try to remove large objects that may be plugging up blood vessels. You could potentially cause much more harm than good, such as internal bleeding.

ANIMAL BITES

From dogs and cats to snakes and bats, any animal with teeth or fangs will bite given the right circumstances. Some may be looking for food, others might be sick, some startled, but many times they're just afraid that you might be a threat. They're trying to protect themselves.

BITES FROM MAMMALS

Mammals include dogs and cats (both domestic and wild), rodents, bears and bats. Bites from mammals can be large or small. Sometimes there are multiple bites, but often, there's only one or two.

Characteristics of Bites from Mammals

- Dirty puncture wounds can be created by teeth.

- Painful bruises can be caused by the force of jaws crushing the tissue.

- Bruising around puncture wounds makes them even more susceptible to bacterial infection.

- Some mammal bites can puncture a bone, in which case the bone also becomes prone to infection.

- Bites that rip flesh are considered gaping wounds and should be treated as such.

How to Treat Bites from Mammals

Treat bites from mammals like you would any other dirty puncture or gaping wound (see page 93).

- Vigorously irrigate the bite with drinkable water (untreated water adds bacteria to the wound); soap; and iodine, peroxide or alcohol, unless you're going to get to a medical facility within an hour.

- Topical honey is a great antibacterial to use directly in the wound, especially if you don't have oral antibiotics. (See page 33; don't use on babies under age two.) If you don't have honey, any antibacterial ointment will do.

- Any of the common antibiotics, such as cephalexin, ciprofloxacin, erythromycin, azithromycin, doxycycline or amoxicillin will help for most bites that start looking infected. (See page 30 for more on getting antibiotics.)

Some bites need additional care.

Harmful Bacteria in Cat Bites

In the world of domestic animal bites, cat bites can be a terror because of the type of bacteria that live in cats' mouths. As many as 15 percent of domestic cat bites can require IV antibiotics to treat the resulting infection.

For any cat bite, vigorously irrigate the wound with clean water. See your doctor if you can. If that's impossible and the wound starts looking infected, begin an oral antibiotic if you have one. If you're not allergic to penicillin, amoxicillin-clavulanate (Augmentin) should be the first choice for antibiotic treatment. In fact, it's a good first choice for any bite. (See page 30 to learn how to get antibiotics in advance.) If you don't have an antibiotic, try pouring honey in the wound (see page 33).

HOW TO TREAT MAMMAL BITES ON THE HAND

Hands have many tissues—such as tendons, tendon coverings (sheaths), bones and joints—that don't have good blood supplies and are close enough to the skin's surface that they're often affected by the bite. If these tissues get infected, it's hard for your blood to supply the tissues with your body's natural defenses against infection—antibodies, white blood cells, etc. Therefore, the infections tend to grow and spread, and can become serious.

For that reason, even if the bite is more of a tear than a puncture wound, if the wound is fairly deep, it's better not to close the skin completely. Instead, clean the wound daily, use a topical antibacterial cream (or honey) and start an oral antibiotic if you have one.

RABIES

Rabies is a virus spread through saliva, which is why it is such a risk with mammal bites. The virus causes brain damage. If you develop rabies, the chance of survival is very slim. Only a handful of people worldwide have ever survived. Avoid any animal exhibiting strange or aggressive behavior.

Many times, an animal that would otherwise shy away can become quite aggressive if it has rabies.

High Rabies Threats
Raccoons
Some rabid animals look sick; others are aggressive—the bite is unprovoked. That's not the case for rabid raccoons. Many people have been bitten by a seemingly healthy, docile raccoon that only bit after the person tried to capture or kill it, and the raccoon turned out to have rabies. If you are bitten by a raccoon, assume it's rabid and get to a medical facility for treatment as soon as possible. If the animal that inflicted the bite can be easily caught without further danger to you or others, do so. But no one should take unnecessary risks.

Bats
Bats have sharp, tiny teeth. You can be bitten by a bat without knowing it or even seeing a wound.

If you come into physical contact with a bat, or if you find a bat in your sleeping area and can't guarantee the bat hasn't bitten you because you've been asleep, you must get a rabies vaccine. People have developed rabies in both of these scenarios.

Spelunkers (cavers) are some of the rare people advised to get a set of pre-exposure rabies vaccines. They've been known to get rabies after being in bat-filled caves (we're talking thousands), even with no direct contact. Rabies is not carried in feces or urine, so it's hypothesized the cavers got it from the dense saliva carried in the air.

The Vaccine
If you're exposed to a bite, even a scratch, from an animal that might have rabies, you should get to a medical clinic if at all possible to see if you need

the vaccine. Depending on the region and the animal, you may have no risk; the animal might need to be penned up for about ten days to watch for signs of rabies; the head might be sent off to a lab to test the brain for rabies; or the risk may be high enough that you need to go ahead and take the vaccine. The vaccine is a series of shots that prompt your body to produce antibodies to kill the virus. Without these immunizations giving your immune system a head start, the rapidly multiplying virus will quickly overwhelm your body's natural defense mechanisms.

People at higher risk for rabies exposure, such as cavers or those who work around wild animals, may opt to get a series of pre-exposure vaccines.

How to Prevent Rabies

There are a few things you can do, with or without the vaccine, to decrease your odds of contracting with rabies.

1. Vigorously clean the wound. Use a little water pressure from a faucet, plastic bag or syringe to squirt the water deep into the wound. You're trying to wash as much virus out of the wound as you can, hoping your body can fight off what remains. (See the section on cleaning a wound, page 98.)

2. In addition, wash the wound with povidone-iodine solution. It kills the virus.

3. Unless the wound is gaping open, don't close it. Keep it open and clean it once or twice a day.

Additional Concerns

1. If the wound gets red or warm or has any other sign of bacterial infection, start antibiotics.

2. Hopefully you're up-to-date on your tetanus shot. The booster lasts ten years.

SNAKES

Venomous snakebites kill several people in the United States every year. A bite can also cause of tissue damage, infections and even loss of limbs.

How to Prevent a Snakebite

As with many potential medical problems, the best treatment is to never have the problem in the first place. There are several things you can do to decrease your risk of a snakebite:

1. **Dress appropriately.** Wear long pants and high-top boots.

2. **Don't tease or play with a snake.** In most instances, don't even try to kill it. Many people get bitten this way. Remember, some snakes can strike up to one-half the length of their bodies. Even if the snake is dead or decapitated, the bite reflex can continue for up to 90 minutes.

3. **Walk away.** Snakes don't want anything to do with you. You're too big to eat. Occasionally, one will get confused and crawl toward you. The fastest they move is around 3 miles (5k) per hour, so it's easy for you to just walk a little faster and escape them.

4. **Watch where you're going and reaching.** Be careful picking up wood, etc. If given the chance, most snakes will crawl away. But if they're startled, they will strike. Whenever possible, wear gloves if you're working with your hands close to the ground.

How to Treat a Snakebite

If you think you've bitten by a venomous snake, get to a medical facility as soon as possible. Antivenom works best if it is given within four hours of the bite. If this means helicopter transfer, so be it. If the bite is on a leg or foot and you have to walk to get help, make a cane out of a tree limb.

SNAKE FACTS

- Most venomous snakes have a triangular-shaped head, but sometimes they can fool you.

- Twenty percent of bites from venomous snakes contain no venom.

- Regardless of all of the above, if severe pain or swelling occurs within minutes of the bite, you can assume venom has been injected.

- Some venomous snakebites don't hurt or swell until hours later, though that's very rare in the United States unless you've been bitten by the Mojave rattlesnake found only in the Mojave desert.

If you can't get to a medical center:

- Clean the bite with soap and drinkable water.

- Keep the bitten extremity at the same level as your heart. If you keep it too high, you might send the venom to your heart faster. If you keep it too low, you might aggravate swelling.

- Take pain medicine if you have it—anything from ibuprofen or acetaminophen to an opiate like codeine or morphine.

- Start IV fluids, if available.

- If an open wound develops, treat it following the directions on page 93.

Don'ts for Snakebites

- Don't cut into the marks. It doesn't help and likely will cause a worsening infection.

- Don't try to suck out the poison, even with instruments made for such. It wastes time and hasn't been shown to help.

- Don't apply ice. It can further damage the tissue.

- Don't use a tourniquet. It damages tissue, and when it's released, you can get a sudden surge of venom.

GUNSHOT WOUNDS

Call 911 and get the victim to medical treatment ASAP. There are all sorts of things that can go wrong. For one thing, if the internal bleeding doesn't stop, surgery may be the only treatment that helps. Also, the victim may need blood transfusions. Neither of these is an option outside a medical facility.

Treating gunshot wounds is complicated and requires advanced knowledge. In the following pages, I've tried to give you an overview so you have the best chance to save a life if you can't get expert medical help, but someone with internal bleeding is probably not going to survive without rapid transfer to a medical facility. Until you can make that transfer, here are some steps to take:

1. **Stop the bleeding.** Direct pressure, elevation and a pressure bandage (see page 93)—in that order—usually work for most extremities.

2. **Treat for shock.** (You should be doing this as you're doing the other steps.) Cover the victim for warmth. Keep him covered unless there's a reason not to, such as while you're checking for wounds (next step).

3. **Strip the person and look over the entire body for wounds.** You can't just depend on looking for an entry and exit wound, thinking you know where the bullet has traveled. Sometimes the bullet can hit a bone, break into fragments and stray anywhere in the body. And some types of bullets can cause multiple injuries.

4. **Remember to cover the person** back up as soon as you can. Death from hypothermia is a real risk.

Signs of Internal Bleeding

Because you can't see internal bleeding, it's important to note the victim's initial vital signs. Warning signs of internal bleeding include:

- decreasing alertness
- nausea/vomiting
- weak pulse
- lowering blood pressure, or faster and faster pulse

What About an IV?

You're probably not going to have one available, but many people have asked me about this at my blog. If you give too much fluid too fast, you may cause the blood pressure to rise enough to blast out blood clots that are keeping the person from bleeding to death. So, unless you're going to transfer to a medical facility soon, forget the IV and concentrate on the other things.

What About the Bullet?

In most circumstances, you don't want to remove an implanted bullet. It's almost impossible to find, and it may actually be corking up a big blood vessel.

Thousands of military members live with shrapnel in their bodies every day. Unless there's initial infection from the wound itself, the body adapts to most metal without much serious problem.

Treatment for a Gunshot Wound to the Head

Don't forget: Ensure the airway is clear and stays clear (see page 43).

- Attempt to control the bleeding with direct pressure as best you can (no tourniquets around the neck).

- Make sure the blood doesn't choke the person. If the person is conscious, sit him up and lean him forward. Turn an unconscious person on his side and bend the top knee forward to keep him that way.

- If you believe a carotid artery (that large artery on either side of the neck that supplies the brain) is nicked, you can apply soft direct pressure and include an occlusive dressing (see the sidebar).

Treatment for a Gunshot Wound to the Chest

Don't forget: Check for and treat sucking wounds (see page 170) and spine injuries (see page 165).

- Open chest wounds are nicknamed sucking chest wounds because as you try to breathe, these wounds suck air in between your lung and your chest wall. That leads to a collapsed lung. You can help stop the sucking by closing the open wound with an occlusive dressing (see the sidebar).

- Remember that the spine is also included in the back of the chest. Be very careful about moving a person who has been shot in the chest. You want to keep the victim as still as possible in case the spinal cord has been hit. (See page 165, on spinal injuries, for more information.)

HOW TO MAKE AN OCCLUSIVE DRESSING USING A DRIVER'S LICENSE

An occlusive dressing is airtight and watertight. Use this type of dressing on a chest wound that involves the lungs. Wounds that involve the lungs typically have visible air bubbles around them, but if you're in doubt about the condition of the lungs, use an occlusive dressing.

One quick way to make an occlusive dressing is to lay a driver's license, credit card or any other small, plastic card on the wound. Be sure to clean the object and wipe away excess blood around the wound. When the person breathes out and the lung gets smaller, this creates a vacuum in the victim's chest that will suck the card onto the wound. But if air needs to escape, it can easily push the object up. Usually the wound is going to ooze a little blood and other fluids that hold the card in place.

You could also use petroleum jelly gauze, or make your own by putting a very thin amount of petroleum jelly on gauze. No petroleum jelly? Try any type of ointment or even honey.

- The victim needs a chest tube right away. The occlusive dressing is just a temporary treatment to keep the situation from getting worse.

- If the heart, lungs, spine or a large blood vessel is damaged, there's not much you can do outside of getting immediate expert medical care.

Treatment for a Gunshot Wound in the Abdomen

Don't forget to protect the victim's organs.

- If the wound is open and you can see the intestines, find a moist, sterile dressing to place on top of the wound (to protect the organs).

- If the intestines are ripped open, the victim needs immediate medical care. If the person doesn't bleed to death, she will likely die of the severe infection that follows this type of injury.

- The victim should take nothing at all by mouth until the pain lets up, and then wait a day or two. This is obviously a difficult situation, but this step is very important. A slow drip of IV fluids would be very useful in this situation.

Treatment for a Gunshot Wound to the Arms or Legs

Don't forget to check the bones for damage.

- Use direct pressure, elevation and a pressure bandage (see page 93)—in that order.

- If an arm wound won't stop bleeding despite direct pressure and elevation above the heart, press on the brachial artery below the armpit. Do this by grabbing underneath the person's upper arm, wrapping your fingers to the artery (located beneath the inner arm) and pressing firmly on it with your fingers. You'll know you probably have it right when the bleeding slows down.

- For a leg wound that won't stop bleeding, apply pressure to the femoral artery. The best place to do this is in the middle of the bend in the muscle between the front of leg and the hip. Use the base of your palm and put all your weight into it.

- If this fails, use a clotting gauze such as QuikClot or Celox, or apply a tourniquet. (It may come down to "lose a limb or lose a life." See page 96 for dos and don'ts of tourniquet use.)

- If the area is rapidly swelling, that's a sign of internal bleeding. Also, consider that a bone might have been injured, even shattered. Try traction (see page 177).

Treatment Tip: To find the brachial artery, here's a trick to try right now: Get a healthy partner who has no circulation problems and who isn't on blood thinners. Find the person's radial pulse (in the wrist on the thumb side). Then grab underneath the upper arm and wrap your fingers to the brachial artery (located beneath the inner arm). You should feel the pulse stop. Only do this for a couple of seconds, of course, because you're stopping blood flow.

BURNS

Burns are most commonly caused by heat, but they can also be caused by chemicals or radiation, to name a couple of other culprits. They are not immediately life threatening unless they:

1. Pose a risk to your airway from damage or swelling of your face or neck, or

2. Involve 10 percent or more of your skin surface. The more area involved, the more urgency there is to see the doctor. You can estimate skin surface area by the rule of nines. Each arm accounts for 9 percent total body surface, as does your face, including the neck. Each leg is 18 percent. The front part of your trunk is 18 percent. So is the back part. The last 1 percent is the genital area.

Memorize this: Limit the damage; cool the burn.

The Rule of Nines

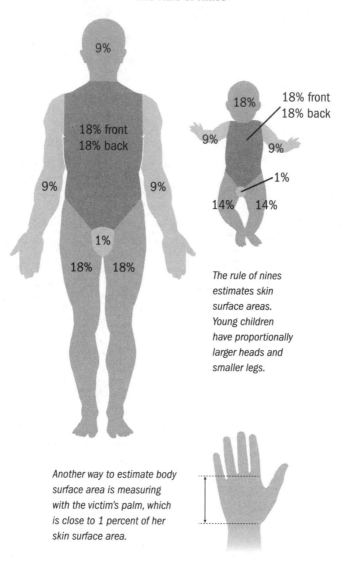

9%

18% front
18% back

9%   9%

1%

18%   18%

18%

18% front
18% back

9%   9%

1%

14%   14%

The rule of nines
estimates skin
surface areas.
Young children
have proportionally
larger heads and
smaller legs.

Another way to estimate body
surface area is measuring
with the victim's palm, which
is close to 1 percent of her
skin surface area.

FIRST STEPS FOR DEALING WITH A BURN

1. Remove any hot or restrictive clothing or jewelry from anywhere on the body, not just at the burn.

2. Run cold water over the affected area. That will wash off the causative agent, unless it's tar. Cold water will also ease the pain and cool down the skin (limiting the damage).

3. Don't use ice as it may constrict needed blood flow to the area.

4. Never use grease, butter or ointments, which may hold the heat in. Tar is the exception. Petroleum jelly will help remove tar without taking the skin with it.

5. Further treatment depends on the surface area and depth of skin damage (degree), as described below.

SIGNS OF A FIRST-DEGREE BURN

- Skin is red and painful.

A mild sunburn is the most common type of first-degree burn. It can be quite the nuisance and very irritating depending on where you are burned.

How to Treat a First-Degree Burn

1. Try cool compresses or aloe vera gel.

2. An anti-inflammatory such as ibuprofen (Advil) or naproxen (Aleve) can help the pain. (Never use aspirin for children. It increases their risk, however rare, of getting a serious disease called Reye's syndrome.)

3. The burn should heal in a few days, and the damaged top layer of skin will slough off—that fun peeling stage that follows a sunburn.

SIGNS OF A SECOND-DEGREE BURN

- The skin blisters (immediately or several hours later) in addition to being red and painful.

Because of the blistering, infection is a possibility with a second-degree burn. These burns usually heal in two or three weeks with minimal scarring, but you need to keep them clean and protected.

How to Treat a Second-Degree Burn

- Leave intact, small blisters alone because they act as a natural sterile bandage.

- Use a sterile instrument (see page 90) to puncture blisters larger than 1 inch (3cm) in diameter because they're probably going to leak anyway. If a blister leaks, it's no longer sterile.

After you puncture a blister or it starts draining on its own:

1. Use tweezers (sterile, if possible) to pull up the loose tissue as you cut it away with scissors.

2. Wash the wound with soap and water; towel dry.

3. Apply antibiotic ointment (or honey, see page 33), gauze and tape.

4. Change the dressing daily or if it gets wet or dirty. Clean off any dirt or crust buildup, then reapply the ointment and bandage.

5. If the redness starts moving into the healthy skin, you have a skin infection and you need an oral antibiotic.

SIGNS OF A THIRD-DEGREE BURN

- These burns go all the way through the skin layers.

- The skin is initially blanched, speckled white or gone.

- Because nerve fibers have been killed, you may not experience as much pain as you have with other burns. The area may even be numb.

How to Treat Third-Degree Burns

1. Third-degree burns need professional medial treatment. If you can't get to a doctor right away, follow the treatment for second-degree burns until you can get to a doctor.

2. Depending on the amount of surface area affected, these burns will take months to heal. Some will never heal without skin grafting. Scarring is inevitable. It's important to keep affected joints as mobile as possible to prevent restrictive scars.

3. Unless you're going to get help within a day or two, the only chance for new healing is to debride (remove) the black, leathery, dead

tissue, called an eschar, that will form. A third-degree burn destroys the layer of skin that produces new skin cells—the layer that allows your skin to grow back. The only skin that is going to grow in an area that received a third-degree burn will be skin from the undamaged outer edges of the burn, so you need to remove the eschar to allow the edges to grow inward and eventually meet.

4. Most third-degree burns that are more than 1 or 2 inches (3 or 5cm) in diameter and go through every layer of skin are going to require skin grafts to heal. Until new skin can be grafted over the burn, keep the burn clean and covered. Infection is the biggest danger.

How to Debride Eschars

An eschar is the dry, leathery remains of dead skin in a third-degree burn. The burn has no chance of healing while the eschar is in place. Debridement should be done in a medical facility, in part because the procedure can leave the person especially prone to infection. If that's not going to be possible for days, be very careful as you attempt the following:

1. Use a sterile scalpel, or sterilize a clean knife.

2. Wash the eschar and the area around it with soap and water.

3. Whittle away. You may have to make a lengthwise cut down the middle if the eschar is thick. It's better to make a cut too shallow than too deep. Don't cut into the living tissue. You can probably judge the depth of the eschar by observation. Cutting away the eschar should not hurt or bleed. The tissue is dead. Living tissue is going to be pink and bleeding. In order to get all the eschar, there may be some light oozing of blood from the living tissue.

4. Apply an antibiotic-soaked (or honey-soaked) dressing when you're finished.

5. Elevate the extremity to cut down on the bleeding and swelling if the burn is to an arm or leg.

6. Change the dressing twice a day.

7. Don't let the burn dry out. It will heal better in a moist environment. The moisture can be from the wound's fluids or antibiotic ointment.

8. At the same time, try to keep the healthy skin around the burn dry. Otherwise, it will get soft and more easily damaged.

LIFE-THREATENING COMPLICATIONS FROM BURNS

Infection

- If the top layer of skin is interrupted, even a crack, there's a risk of infection. The deeper the burn and the more skin area involved, the higher the risk of infection.

- To prevent infection, you must keep the area clean by gently washing it with soap and water. This is essential, but fair warning: It's going to hurt.

- Keep the burn area moist with an antibiotic ointment or honey and an absorbent dressing. It will heal quicker if it stays moist. Change the dressing once or twice a day.

- Many times a yellowish film forms over a healing burn. A little of this film is okay, but sometimes it's hard to tell this film from infection. An infected area usually oozes, and the skin around the wound becomes warm and red. If you have a doubt, or if the film seems to be getting thicker, it's time to vigorously clean the wound—or even debride it by lifting and cutting the yellow film with sterile tweezers and scissors.

Start antibiotics (see page 31) if you:

- see pus in the burn or redness spreading around it

- see red streaks

- run a fever

If you don't have antibiotics, apply mupirocin ointment or honey to the burn.

Swelling

One of the functions of the skin is to retain, or store, tissue fluids. Damaged, burned flesh causes the smallest blood vessels (capillaries) to ooze lots of fluid (usually not blood cells, which are bigger than the leaks). This can cause dramatic swelling in the surrounding tissue.

- Swelling is a major reason face and neck burns can be so serious. If the swelling is too severe, it can interfere with a person's breathing and even block an airway.

- In an arm or leg, swelling can cut off the blood supply to a hand or foot. Any living tissue that is denied blood flow will eventually die.

How to Treat Swelling

- To minimize or avoid swelling, keep the affected area elevated at heart level or above. Avoid restrictive clothing or jewelry. Don't tightly bandage the area.

Dehydration

- Burned tissue cannot retain tissue fluid, so the fluid seeps out into areas of the body where it does not belong and does more harm than good.

- If the burn involves 10 percent or more of the body surface area, cells all over the victim's body start leaking, not just in the burned area. The person must drink a lot of liquids to avoid dehydration. He needs to get medical help as soon as possible.

- The best replacement fluid is Pedialyte or a sports drink like Gatorade. An alternative is a ½ teaspoon (2.5g) of salt and a ½ teaspoon (2.5g) of baking soda in a quart (liter) of water.

- If 10 percent or so of the body surface is burned, drink a minimum of 4 quarts (1 gallon; 4L) of fluid a day. Add a quart (liter) for every percent of burned surface over 10. If the burn area is 20 percent or more, the victim will require special IV fluids.

SIX

REACTIONS: ANAPHYLAXIS, SKIN IRRITATIONS AND POISONING

Unless you happen to be in the polar regions, you can count on having to deal with some sort of insect or plant that seems to be around for the sole purpose of causing you misery. You know, poison ivy, wasps, scorpions, ticks... If you have a run-in with one, you could have a dangerous (sometimes deadly) reaction, get a disease or even get infected from incessantly scratching an itch in unsanitary conditions.

The most obvious suggestion is to avoid these creatures, or at least make yourself a less likable target. In this chapter, I'll give you tips on how to do that. But sometimes, despite your best efforts, you'll meet one of these undesirables up close. So, I'll also tell you some things you can do in those situations.

ANAPHYLAXIS: A POTENTIALLY DEADLY REACTION

Coming into contact with any of the insects and plants in this chapter can cause the serious and often deadly reaction called anaphylaxis. (Nuts, latex, medications, pollens and just about anything you come into contact with also can cause anaphylaxis.) Fortunately this reaction is rare.

Some people get warnings that they're at risk for anaphylaxis, like breaking out in hives. But that's not always the case. Even if you've rolled around in poison ivy or had a swarm of bees sting you with no problem, the next time you have the slightest contact could be your last. That's not to scare you. It's only to prepare you.

Anaphylaxis occurs anywhere from a few seconds to two hours after contact with whatever caused the reaction. Except for hives (which are more of a warning sign), the effects of anaphylaxis center around the respiratory and cardiovascular systems. Your airways swell or your cardiovascular system collapses, or both.

Signs and Symptoms of Anaphylaxis

Common signs and symptoms of anaphylaxis include the following (you may have any or all of these signs):

- raised and itchy hives, or welts, which can break out anywhere on the body

- swelling of the face, tongue or throat

- trouble breathing

- dizziness

- heart beating really fast

- a tingling or funny taste in your mouth

- an overwhelming feeling of anxiety or impending doom

How to Treat Anaphylaxis

Call 911. If you can't call for help, get to the nearest medical clinic as soon as possible.

In addition to seeking professional medical help, do one of the following, listed in order of effectiveness:

1. **Inject epinephrine.** This is the medicine of choice for treating anaphylaxis. Nothing works as fast or is as effective. Everyone should have an autoinjector of epinephrine (EpiPen) in his backpack or bug out bag. They make a children's dose also (EpiPen Jr).

2. **Take an antihistamine.** Diphenhydramine (Benadryl) is best. If you don't have that, take one of the nondrowsy types like loratadine (Claritin) or cetirizine (Zyrtec).

3. **Use a bronchodilator.** An albuterol inhaler used for asthma attacks can help the victim's breathing if injectable epinephrine is not available. It works similar to epinephrine, but only on the airways.

4. **Take a steroid.** Take an oral prednisone or something similar if you have it available. (This medication is available by prescription only.) It works well but takes several hours to go into effect. The usual dosage is about 60mg for an adult and 1mg for every 2.2 lbs (1kg) in a child. Taper down the dosage by 10mg (or a similar proportion for a child) every day thereafter.

THE EPIPEN

An EpiPen is a brand name autoinjector of epinephrine. It includes a single dosage of epinephrine, which is used to stop anaphylaxis reactions. People who suffer from severe food allergies often carry this device with them at all times. I consider it a necessity for any bug out bag or survival first aid kit. EpiPens are available by prescription only, so you will need to ask your doctor for a prescription. Also be sure to read the instructions on how to use it before you need it. Review the instructions whenever you update the contents of your first aid kit, and keep them with the EpiPen.

5. **Try a stomach medicine.** Cimetidine (Tagamet), famotidine (Pepcid) and ranitidine (Zantac) are special types of over-the-counter antihistamines and worth a try.

If you take an oral medicine to treat anaphylaxis, continue taking it for at least three days, just to be safe.

How to Prevent Anaphylaxis

If you've had a severe allergic reaction to something in the past, you have a high chance of having another severe reaction with your next contact. (With bees, your chances of a second severe reaction is somewhere around 30 to 60 percent.) Therefore, you should get allergy testing and shots by an allergist. It's a great way to prepare. Don't delay.

REACTIONS

STINGING INSECTS

Stinging insects include bees, wasps, fire ants and scorpions. Reactions and treatment for these types of stings and bites are similar, so I will cover them together in this section. The exception is the bark scorpion, which has its own section.

Bees and Wasps

- If you are stung by a bee, brush off the stinger from your skin immediately.

- Don't pinch the stinger because that will squeeze venom into your skin.

One main difference between being stung by a wasp and being stung by a bee is the same wasp can sting you multiple times, but a bee will sting only one time. That makes wasps pretty bad to be around. But sting for sting, bees can be worse. A bee has a barb on the end of its stinger. When the bee stings, the stinger and a venom sac attached to it may break away from the bee and stay in your skin. The sac continues to pump venom into your skin for up to a minute after detaching from the bee, which is why you want to get that stinger out as quickly as possible. We used to think scraping away a stinger with a credit card was great, but unless the card is already in your hand, that method takes too long. While you're finding a card, that venom sac is pumping away.

Fire Ants

- They started in the Southeast, then spread to the Southwest, California and along the Atlantic coast, but they're headed northward.

- They can also be found on trees, feeding on creatures and even on top of water.

- Their mounds are much larger than other ant mounds.

- They're not the largest ants, but they're the most aggressive.

- They clamp onto you with their pincers and swing their tails around for multiple stings.

- It can take some vigorous brushing to release the grip of their bite.

Reactions to Insect Stings

Local reactions to a sting from a bee, wasp, fire ant or scorpion can be any or all of the following:

- an itchy bump

- a welt

- a major swelling of an affected extremity

- anaphylaxis (see page 131).

Infections

The local reaction can cause swelling, redness and warmth around the sting that is hard to differentiate from an infection. A sign that points toward infection would be if the area didn't have these problems until a day or two after. Other signs include fever, red streaks, pus or tender, swollen lymph nodes in the armpit or groin. If in doubt, start antibiotics, if available (see page 31). If not, using honey (see page 33) may help.

How to Treat a Sting

- Clean the area immediately. Anytime the skin is pierced, there is a real risk for infection. This is especially true with fire ants because their stings itch. Scratching can further expose the skin to bacteria.

REACTIONS

- Use any of the recommended home remedies to relieve pain and swelling.

- Leave any blisters intact. After a day or two, fire ant stings can result in tiny, cloudy blisters. That's not pus in them. It's dead skin. The fire ant wounds heal faster and are less prone to infection if the blisters are kept intact.

- Treat leaking blisters as you would treat any open wound, with daily cleaning, antibacterial ointment and bandaging.

Home Remedies for Stings

After cleaning the sting, apply any of these remedies right away:

- paste of baking soda and water

- vinegar

- paste of baking soda and vinegar

- meat tenderizer

- wet tobacco

- tea tree oil

BARK SCORPION

- lives in the Southwest United States

- measures about 2 to 3 inches (5 to 8cm) in length

- is grayish or yellowish, usually with no stripes

- is fluorescent yellow in the dark, under a black (Wood's) light

- often hides in shoes, clothes or blankets, or under ground coverings

- likes to live in trees (hence its name) and under fallen trees, in woodpiles or in any dark crevice

Reactions to a Bark Scorpion Sting
Reactions usually occur within minutes. Serious symptoms include:

- blurred vision

- increased saliva

- tongue twitching

- trouble swallowing

- trouble breathing

- muscle twitching or jerking

The bark scorpion sting can be lethal, but that's rare. In fact, most cause no more problems than other insect stings, especially in adults. The sting is much more likely to be serious in children under age five, adults age 65 or older, or people with a chronic illness.

How to Treat a Bark Scorpion Sting
If the person stung by a bark scorpion falls in the high-risk category (under age five, age 65 or older, or chronically ill) or starts having serious symptoms, call 911 or get her to a medical facility for support not available in the field.

If help is not available, the person should lie down and get as comfortable as possible. Give her a muscle relaxer or minor sedative for the muscle jerks. Prednisone is worth a try.

Otherwise, treat as you would a bee or wasp sting (see page 134).

REACTIONS

SPIDERS

Most spider bites are harmless and unnoticeable. Some can cause local allergic reactions that respond to antihistamines. As with any bite, the area can get infected, so be sure to clean and apply antibiotic ointment to any bite marks. In the United States, there are three venomous spiders to worry about: the black widow, the brown recluse and the hobo spider.

Black Widow Spider

Black widows typically have some sort of red marking on their abdomens, but not always. The marking is usually shaped like an hourglass.

These spiders live under eaves and around undisturbed debris, woodpiles, porch furniture, barns, sheds and outhouses.

Signs and Symptoms of a Black Widow Bite

If you are bitten by a black widow spider, you may experience some or all of these symptoms:

- painful bite (but not always)

- two tiny fang marks, possibly a little red mark, maybe some swelling (but sometimes there's no evidence of the bite)

- muscle aches and cramping of the abdomen, back and extremities that can be severe

- increased sweating or salivation

- elevated blood pressure

- rarely, seizures or respiratory difficulties that can result in death, usually in children

- symptoms usually peak within about 12 hours but can continue for several days

The black widow spider. Not every black widow has such a notable hourglass marking.

How to Treat a Black Widow Bite

- Apply cold packs to the bite area intermittently for five- to ten-minute intervals. (Place a cloth between the pack and the skin.)

- Call the regional poison control office for advice. Its number should be on your speed dial. Find the number for your regional office at www.aapcc.org.

- Seek medical care, if possible. There is an antivenom for those who develop severe symptoms.

- Wash the bite area with soap and water, and apply an antibacterial ointment.

- Take whatever you have for the pain. Often, strong narcotics are needed.

Brown Recluse Spider

Brown recluses are characterized by a violin-shaped marking on their backs. They like to live in dark, secluded areas—under rocks, under wood and in undisturbed storage areas.

REACTIONS

The brown recluse is also known as the fiddleback spider.

Signs and Symptoms of a Brown Recluse Bite

- The bite causes little or no pain.

- Within minutes to hours, skin irritation and damage can cause increasing pain.

- Skin redness may develop.

- Dead tissue may cause a black spot in the middle of the redness. As more tissue dies, the black spot grows (as does the pain).

How to Treat a Brown Recluse Bite

- Apply cold packs to the bite area intermittently for five- to ten-minute intervals. (Place a cloth between the pack and the skin.)

- Take whatever pain reliever you have on hand.

- Wash the bite area with soap and water. Keep the wound clean.

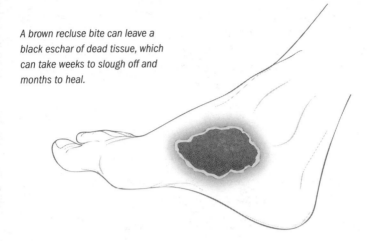

A brown recluse bite can leave a black eschar of dead tissue, which can take weeks to slough off and months to heal.

- As the black layer of dead skin (eschar) sloughs off, treat the wound as you would any other flesh wound—by keeping it clean and covered and applying antibiotic ointment or honey. Some large wounds take several weeks to heal. If it starts looking infected, you'll need oral antibiotics.

Hobo Spider
This brown spider has yellow markings on its abdomen. The symptoms from its bite are similar to those from a brown recluse bite but usually not as severe. Treat the bite as you would treat a bite from a brown recluse.

MOSQUITO BITES
In most species of mosquitoes, the females need a bit of blood to develop their eggs. Skin makeup, carbon dioxide output and other factors can make some people more appealing to mosquitoes than others. But don't feel too left out. If you're available for biting, mosquitoes will likely give anyone a few tries.

REACTIONS

When a mosquito bites you, it first pierces your skin with a long, skinny funnel that is attached to its mouth. Then, it secretes tiny bits of saliva, which contains proteins that make your blood easier to suck through the funnel. These proteins are what cause the allergic reaction (itching) a person experiences in response to a mosquito bite.

Reactions to a Mosquito Bite

- itchy bump (a local allergic reaction common in almost everyone)

- large welts, blisters, swelling or redness (less common, but some people do experience this more severe reaction)

- anaphylactic reaction (though it's extremely rare)

How to Treat Mosquito Bites

- Treatment is the same as for stinging insects (see page 134).

- Try not to scratch, as this increases your risk of infection.

- To relieve the itching, try cold packs, hydrocortisone cream, calamine lotion, tea tree oil or an oral antihistamine such as diphenhydramine (Benadryl).

DISEASES TRANSMITTED BY MOSQUITOES

In addition to being annoying and itchy, bites from mosquitoes can cause serious viral infections. There is no cure for these viruses except trying to stay healthy and hydrated long enough for the disease to run its course. But there are methods that protect you from being exposed to the bite in the first place. The methods are outlined in the "How to Prevent Parasitic Insect Bites" section (page 152) in this chapter.

Malaria

Malaria is caused by a parasite found in the saliva of infected mosquitos. The mosquito bite transfers the parasite into a human's bloodstream. It's most commonly found in tropical and subtropical regions near the equator. Although malaria mosquitoes have been eliminated in the United States, an average of 1,500 Americans get the disease by visiting other countries where it's still rampant. Rarely, a mosquito may bite one of these people and infect someone else. Special medication, depending on the type of parasite causing the malaria, is used to treat the disease.

Symptoms of Malaria

- fever

- moderate to severe shaking chills

- profuse sweating after the chills

How to Prevent Malaria

- Prescription medication taken prior to being exposed can prevent it. This is recommended for anyone traveling to a region affected by the disease.

- Barrier methods like mosquito netting work well.

- Follow the recommendations for preventing parasitic bites (see page 152).

West Nile Virus

In the past few years, West Nile virus has been the most prevalent mosquito-borne virus in the United States. It becomes a risk in summer and fall months, and some years are worse than others.

Symptoms of West Nile Virus

About 80 percent of those infected with West Nile virus never know they have it. They never have symptoms and have no known long-term complications.

About 20 percent have a flu-like virus that lasts three to six days. Symptoms may include:

- fever

- fatigue

- poor appetite

- eye pain

- headache

- muscle ache

- nausea

- vomiting

- rash

- swollen lymph glands

How to Treat West Nile Virus

The treatment is the usual for a virus:

- rest

- lots of fluids

- symptom relief for nausea, fever, etc.

West Nile Encephalitis

Around one out of every 150 people infected with West Nile virus develops West Nile encephalitis. The signs and symptoms include:

- fever
- intestinal symptoms
- change in mental function
- sometimes a rash

Other possible symptoms include:

- severe muscle weakness
- paralysis
- trouble with balance
- nerve damage
- seizures

For West Nile encephalitis, hospitalization is essential to support the respiratory system and to give IV fluids. If medical help is impossible, all you can do is follow the treatment for the flu-like virus, but expect a mortality rate well above 20 percent. Those who do make it are in for a long convalescence and have a high risk for permanent brain damage.

Other Mosquito-Borne Viruses

The rest of the diseases mosquitoes carry are also viruses. Examples are:

- dengue fever
- Saint Louis encephalitis
- eastern and western equine encephalitis

There are no specific vaccines or antiviral medicines for these diseases. Fortunately, many of the viruses cause a few days to weeks of flu-like symptoms and resolve on their own. However some people can get much sicker and even die from complications like encephalitis and meningitis. These people require full hospital support with IV fluids, oxygen and supportive injectable medication if they are to pull through.

TICKS

If you're outside, check yourself for ticks every few hours. The sooner you remove the tick, the better. At the end of the day, thoroughly check your clothes and yourself. Ticks can be tiny and hidden. Check your hair, under your arms, your belly button, private areas—every nook and cranny. The sooner you remove a tick, the less likely it is to infect you with whatever it's carrying.

How to Remove a Tick

The best way to remove a tick is with a pair of tweezers (the thinner the ends, the better).

1. Grasp the tick at its head with the tweezers. Plucking the tick by its body will squeeze the stomach contents into your skin and increase your risk of a transmitted infection.

2. Pull away from the skin with a steady force. Jerking or twisting increases the risk of the head and pincers breaking off and staying stuck in the skin. If that happens, try to remove them with the tweezers. If you can't, don't worry too much. The head may cause a local skin infection, but it alone won't transmit the serious diseases.

Do Not:

- Apply nail polish, petroleum jelly or the like to the tick. This prolongs the time the tick is attached compared to pulling it off with tweezers. Also, coating the tick can possibly cause the tick to regurgitate its stomach contents into your skin.

- Use heat (a match head) to draw out the tick. Again, this can possibly cause the tick to regurgitate its stomach contents.

DISEASES TRANSMITTED BY TICKS

According to the Centers for Disease Control and Prevention (CDC), ticks can transmit 12 known specific infections to humans. Know which infections are prevalent in your area. An easy way to find out is to go to the website CDC.gov and search for "tick diseases." Two common diseases transmitted by ticks are Lyme disease and Rocky Mountain spotted fever.

Lyme Disease

Lyme disease is the most common tick-borne infection in North America and Europe. About 60 percent of people who have an untreated case of Lyme disease develop permanent, intermittent joint swelling and pain, and about 5 percent develop shooting nerve pain and muscle weakness. Some can also develop heart irregularities. About 20 percent of people with Lyme disease have muscle and joint symptoms, headaches or trouble thinking clearly for many months. Taking longer doses of antibiotics doesn't help. The symptoms finally go away with time.

Symptoms of Lyme Disease

- Flu-like symptoms such as fever and muscle aches start three to 30 days after a bite.

- A rash develops about 70 percent of the time. The rash is typically a "target" or "bull's-eye" lesion, with a red center surrounded by a lighter area, then a red perimeter. The lesion can be anywhere from a few inches (centimeters) to a foot (30cm) in diameter.

How to Treat Lyme Disease

Lyme disease is treated with prescription antibiotics. Whether or not you find a tick, if it's spring or summer and you're in a high-risk area and you develop the rash, fever or other symptoms (muscle aches, etc.), see your doctor, who will likely prescribe doxycycline 100mg twice a day for 14 to 21 days. Amoxicillin is an alternative for those who are allergic to doxycycline, women who are pregnant or breast-feeding and children under age eight. If you're allergic to penicillin, cefuroxime (Ceftin) is an alternative, as are erythromycin, azithromycin and clarithromycin, again taken for 14 to 21 days.

If you can't get expert help and you have doxycycline on hand, consider taking one dose of 100mg within 72 hours of finding the tick to prevent the disease if the following two criteria are met:

- You find an attached tick that may have been on you for 36 hours or longer.

- You're in an area that has a high risk for Lyme disease, and you have the antibiotic.

Rocky Mountain Spotted Fever

Rocky Mountain spotted fever is transmitted by a few specific tick species including the American dog tick, Rocky Mountain wood tick and brown dog tick. Ticks that carry the disease can transmit it within as few as two hours after attaching to a person.

Symptoms of Rocky Mountain Spotted Fever

Symptoms can start anywhere from two to 14 days after receiving the tick bite and include:

- fever

- headaches

- abdominal pain

- a red, spotted rash that starts about two to five days after the fever beginning on the hands and arms and may spread to the body

How to Treat Rocky Mountain Spotted Fever

Trying to prevent Rocky Mountain spotted fever by taking antibiotics before symptoms develop has not been shown to help.

If you live in a high-risk area, visit your doctor immediately if you develop any of the symptoms, whether or not you find a tick on you. Without treatment, the overall risk of dying is 20 percent. With proper treatment, the risk drops to around 5 percent. Hospitalization is often required due to kidney or nerve damage.

If you have the symptoms, you're in a high-risk area and it's tick season but you can't get to a doctor right away, take the antibiotic doxycycline 100mg twice a day for two weeks if you have it. If the infected person is under 100 pounds (45kg), the dose is 2.2mg of doxycycline per 1 kg (2.2 lbs) of body weight twice a day. Doxycycline is likely to cause permanently stained teeth in children under age eight, and chloramphenicol (which has its own set of problems) can be used for milder cases, but no antibiotic has been proven to decrease mortality as well as doxycycline.

Other than antibiotics, the treatment is supportive, such as rest and fluids.

FLEAS

Fleas are most likely to live on other mammals, but they will bite and feed on humans. You may encounter hungry fleas if you try to stay in a shelter recently vacated by a flea-infested mammal.

You may see fleas on your body, but more likely the itching that results from the bite will first alert you to their presence. For a better look, wait until dark

REACTIONS

and shine a light parallel to the floor. Chances are, you'll discover a bunch of hopping little dots.

Reaction to a Flea Bite

- The bumps from the bites can range from very small to large. If you have a local allergic reaction to them, they'll also be itchy.

- They tend to be on the lower legs if you're walking or standing on the floor where the fleas are.

- The bites can range from one to several and are random. They have no distinct pattern.

How to Treat a Flea Bite

Treat the symptoms like you would any other insect bite or sting (see page 134).

Plague Transmitted by Fleas

Every year, there are a few cases of the plague in the United States. The cases are caused by bites from infected fleas that usually live on rodents. There are three types of plague, all with fever and weakness—all potentially fatal. You can have more than one type.

- Bubonic plague causes tender, swollen lymph nodes (called buboes) in the groin or armpits.

- Septicemic plague causes areas of the skin, fingers, toes or nose to turn black, die and slough off (called gangrene).

- Pneumonic plague causes shortness of breath, chest pain and a cough—sometimes bloody. Pneumonic can be spread to other people by droplets from the cough. It is the most lethal type of plague.

Treatment

Early treatment with antibiotics (preferably IV), such as tetracycline, doxycycline, ciprofloxacin or others, can cut the overall mortality risk to 13 percent. The lowest risk of death occurs with the bubonic type. The highest risk of death, approaching 100 percent if antibiotics are not started within 24 hours, is with the pneumonic type. Any of the types can be prevented by giving a week of the antibiotics to any nonsymptomatic person who might have been exposed to the fleas or come in close contact with a person with pneumonic plague.

Without antibiotics, the overall mortality rate is around 50 percent. Other than antibiotics, the treatment is supportive—fluids, rest, etc.

CHIGGERS

These are tiny larvae of mites. They like to hang out in thick, shaded vegetation. They feed on animal proteins and are attracted to the carbon dioxide exhaled by humans and other animals. The good news is they don't carry any known human diseases. Instead, their bites cause intense itching.

Treatment Tip: Chiggers do not burrow under the skin. The tiny red spot they leave is a breakdown of skin tissue. When they feed, they insert a funnel and release enzymes that dissolve tissue, which they suck up. They can stay put and feed like this for several days.

How to Treat Chigger Bites

- Search for and wash or brush off any chiggers. They like to congregate in skin folds and around tight bands of clothing (under socks, waistbands, etc.).

- Washing in warm water dislodges the chiggers.

- Treat as you would other insect bites (see page 134).

- To relieve the itching, try hydrocortisone cream, calamine lotion, tea tree oil or an oral antihistamine such as diphenhydramine (Benadryl).

HOW TO PREVENT PARASITIC INSECT BITES

While antibiotics can be used to treat some infections transmitted by parasitic insects, there is no cure for viral infections transmitted by these parasites. If you contract a virus, all you can do is try to stay healthy and hydrated long enough for the disease to run its course.

Prevention, of course, is the best treatment. So your best option is to avoid being bitten by a parasite. The following methods will protect you from being exposed to a bite (and they also help prevent chigger bites):

Barrier Methods for Preventing Insect Bites

- Wear hats and boots, especially in wooded areas and high grass. Consider long-sleeved shirts and long pants.

- Tuck your shirt in, and tuck your pants into your socks or boots.

- Consider sleeping under netting.

- Wear light-colored clothes so ticks, chiggers, fleas, etc. are easier to see and brush off.

Chemical Insect Repellants for Parasitic Insects

With all of these repellants, use as directed and be sure to read up on precautions, side effects and use on children. Avoid getting them in the mouth or eyes. To apply repellant to your face, put it on your hands and rub on your face. Rub the repellant on children rather than spraying it on them. Wash your hands after applying to avoid getting it in your eyes.

- **DEET.** Apply to exposed skin, clothes, bed nets, etc. For protection that lasts more than a couple of hours, use a product with a concentration of at least 10 percent. Concentrations over 50 percent offer no added benefit.

- **Picaridin.** Found in Skin So Soft, among other commercial brands.

- **Permethrin.** To be used on clothing, bed nets and camping gear to repel mosquitoes. Some clothing comes pretreated. (It also treats scabies when applied to skin as directed.)

Natural Insect Repellants
Remember, just because something is natural doesn't mean it's not harmful. Again, use as directed and be sure to read up on precautions, side effects and use on children. Avoid getting them in the mouth or eyes. The following can be found on the Web or at many health food stores:

- neem oil

- geraniol

- lemon eucalyptus oil

- citronella (Putting out the plant or burning a candle containing the oil repels mosquitoes to some degree.)

POISON IVY, POISON OAK AND POISON SUMAC

How to Prevent a Reaction to Poison Ivy
The best way to prevent having a reaction to poison ivy, poison oak or poison sumac is to avoid the plants. This is good advice even for those who have never had an adverse reaction to these plants. New allergies can

Poison ivy

develop at any time, and if you do become allergic, from then on, you'll always be allergic.

The problem with avoidance is it can be tougher than it seems. You don't even have to directly touch these sneaky plants to get attacked. Urushiol, the oil in the plants that causes the allergic reaction, can get on your clothes or on your pet's fur, or even float in the air.

Tips for Avoiding Poison Ivy

1. **Know what it looks like.** "Leaves of three, let them be." I know you've heard this saying before, but you really want to know what these plants look like. Skin-irritating plants come in three main varieties: ivy (looks like a weed), oak (a vine) and sumac (a woody shrub). Of course, other non-allergy-causing plants can look very similar, but unless you know your plants really, really well, I suggest not taking chances.

2. **Don't trust dormant plants.** In the winter the "leaves of three" axiom is not going to help because there are no leaves. But the dormant vines, stems and roots all contain the urushiol that causes the allergic reaction.

3. **Wash yourself and your clothes.** As soon as you return from being in the woods or working in your yard, take off your clothes and wash them right away. Your clothes, particularly your pants, shoes and socks, may have picked up urushiol. Wash yourself with water and plenty of soap. Yes, the oil can spread by rubbing, but using soap along with the water will clean it off your skin.

4. **Wash your pets.** Wear gloves when you bathe your furry pal so the urushiol doesn't transfer to your skin. Even if you use gloves, you'll probably want to wash yourself well afterward, just in case.

Prevention Tip: Burning poison ivy, poison oak and poison sumac releases urushiol, the oil in the plant that causes the allergic reaction, into the air. Any exposed skin that comes into contact with the oil in the air may react. Inhaled smoke can expose the lung linings to the oil. If this causes severe shortness of breath, it should be treated as an anaphylactic reaction (see page 131). Be very careful not to include these "poisonous" plants in piles of weeds or lawn clippings that you burn.

If Think You've Come in Contact with Poison Ivy

- Wash potentially exposed skin with soap and water within ten minutes of contact.

- Rubbing alcohol is better than just water if you don't have soap. You can also buy "poison ivy soap," which is a cleanser specifically designed to remove urushiol from your skin.

If you can remove the urushiol within ten minutes, your chances of prevention are very good. Longer than that, and the urushiol starts binding to your skin. It's probably completely bound within an hour, but even washing within four hours may help you some.

Signs and Symptoms of Poison Ivy

- a rash—normally red and raised, with blisters

The rash usually occurs in the spots where you've come in contact with the plant or oil. Rarely, some rashes start with contact and spread to other parts of your body. Don't think the open blisters or soap you use has spread it, though. Blisters don't spread the oil. Rather, this diffuse rash is the result of a more severe, systemic allergic reaction you're having. The treatments for both the direct contact and diffuse rashes are the same.

How to Treat Poison Ivy

There is no cure or vaccine. The best you can hope for is to shorten the duration of the rash and alleviate some of the itching.

Prescriptions

A steroid shot or course of oral steroids, or both, may help—even shorten the duration of the rash. (No matter what, you're likely in for a few days to a couple of weeks of misery.) You might also get a stronger steroid cream from your doctor.

Over-the-Counter Treatments

- Hydrocortisone cream may help the inflammation and itching. The strongest you can get over the counter is 1 percent.

- Calamine lotion may help the itching. Don't get Caladryl lotion because it can cause a separate allergic reaction.

JEWELWEED: A NATURAL POISON IVY TREATMENT

Jewelweed typically grows in the same areas as poison ivy. The leaves and stems contain a gel that helps counteract the urushiol. Know what jewelweed looks like. If you get into some poison ivy, oak or sumac, grab a bunch of jewelweed, crush it up, stems and all, and smear it on your skin. But still wash the area well with water and soap as soon as possible.

Jewelweed

REACTIONS

- Oral antihistamines like diphenhydramine (Benadryl) ease the itching but can make you drowsy (which sometimes is a good thing, especially if the itching is keeping you from falling asleep).

Other Treatments

- Jewelweed soap can help if used early.

- Witchhazel, an astringent, can help dry the rash.

- Quercetin drops have anti-inflammatory effects and can be taken orally and rubbed on the rash.

- Aloe vera can soothe.

- Cool baths, cool compresses and oatmeal baths can help the itching.

- Tea tree oil can decrease the reaction and help prevent secondary infection.

Treatment Tip: Here's a poison ivy treatment you may not know: If you've tried the other treatments and the itching is still driving you crazy, try getting in the shower with the water as hot as you can stand it. (Obviously don't burn your skin.) Apparently this depletes your body's supply of itch-causing histamines and can give you relief for a few hours.

STINGING NETTLES

Some people boil the plant for medicinal purposes, but beware of touching it with your bare skin. The tiny, hair-like spines that cover the plant inject chemicals into the skin that can cause intense stinging similar to many small bee stings. Immediately wash the affected skin with water, alcohol, or whatever you have handy. If you start having welts, swelling, shortness of breath or other symptoms of an anaphylactic reaction, treat it as such (see page 131).

CACTUS

In the Southwest, it's not unusual to touch or even fall into a cactus. Multiple tiny spines can stick into your skin and be difficult to remove. They cause serious irritation from inflammation and may cause infection.

How to Remove Cactus Spines

- Pluck out the larger spines with tweezers.

- To remove small spines, place some adhesive tape over the affected skin. When you peel off the tape, many of the little spines will come off with it. Repeat until you think you have them all.

How to Treat Skin Irritated by Cactus

- Wash the affected area with soap and water.

- To soothe the irritation, soak a large cloth with an aluminum acetate solution, such as Domeboro or Burow's Solution, and apply to the affected area for 20 minutes or so. Repeat often. The solutions are widely available over the counter.

INGESTING POISONOUS PLANTS

Sure, there are plenty of great, edible wild plants to sustain you when you can't get to the grocery store, but this section is concerned with what to do if you happen to eat the wrong ones—the kinds that can make you awfully sick. Because many poisonous plants, mushrooms and berries resemble their nutritious neighbors, I suggest you know your plants extremely well before munching down. Consult a field guide such as *A Field Guide to Edible Wild Plants of Eastern and Central North America* by Lee Allen Peterson. Even then, if the plant is growing near the highway or a factory, it may be contaminated with various toxins such as mercury and insecticides.

REACTIONS

Signs and Symptoms of Ingesting a Poisonous Plant

In general, plant poisons most often affect one of three body systems:

1. **gastrointestinal system:** marked by abdominal pain, vomiting, fever

2. **nervous system:** marked by dry mouth, blurred vision, increased saliva, hallucinations, seizures

3. **cardiovascular system:** marked by irregular, fast or slow heart rate; high or low blood pressure

How to Treat Poisoning by Plants

Know what the person ate. Keep a sample with you if possible. There are specific treatments depending on the plant.

- Call 911. (The sooner you call, the better).

- Get expert medical help as soon as possible.

- Call your regional poison control center. Have the number on speed dial. Find the number for your regional office at www.aapcc.org.

Induce Vomiting If:

- you can't get to or call for medical help

- less than two hours have passed since the plant was ingested

Inducing vomiting is not recommended nearly as much as it was in the past. For one thing, we have no real study-proven evidence it helps.

Never Induce Vomiting If:

- you've ingested something you think may be irritating to the throat

- you're drowsy (you're more likely to choke on the vomited fluids if you're not alert)

Ways to Induce Vomiting

1. **Ipecac**, the most reliable method to induce vomiting. The dosage is:

    - 2 tablespoons (30ml) followed by a quart (liter) of water

    - For children age six and under: 1 tablespoon (14ml) followed by a ½ quart (½ liter) of water depending on size

2. **Soap:** Add a teaspoon (5ml) of soap to a quart (liter) of water.

3. **Activated charcoal:** This is another method that may or may not help, but it's worth a try if you can't get expert help or advice. Use as directed on the packaging.

Support

- Limit the symptoms by trying to stay hydrated (see page 49).

- Take any known antidote.

- Make sure the airway stays open. If the person is lying down in a deep sleep, turn him on his side and prop the person up so he stays in that position (see page 43).

REACTIONS

SEVEN

BONES AND JOINTS

If you're camping or hiking or doing any sort of activity outside, an injured bone or joint is one of the most frequent and debilitating injuries you'll encounter. And, yes, these types of injuries can happen indoors, as well.

DEFINITIONS

Anatomy

Ligament: A strong strip of fibrous tissue that attaches one bone to another bone to hold them together.

Tendon: A strong strip of fibrous tissue that attaches a muscle to a bone, usually crossing over a joint. When the muscle contracts or relaxes, the joint moves.

Types of Injuries

Fracture, broken bone, cracked bone: All the same thing.

Open, or compound, fracture: A broken bone that has torn through the skin. It doesn't matter if the bone is sticking out of the skin or only poked out for a millisecond. With this type of fracture, the risk of the bone becoming infected is very high.

Sprain: One or more injured ligaments. The ligament can be stretched, torn, partially torn or ripped completely away from one of the bones.

Strain: One or more injured muscles or tendons. The tendon or muscle can be stretched, torn or partially torn, or the tendon can be ripped (avulsed) from the attached bone.

RICES TREATMENT FOR BONE, MUSCLE AND JOINT INJURY

Remember the acronym RICES (Rest, Ice, Compression, Elevation, Splint) when treating an injured bone, muscle or joint. This basic treatment does the following:

1. It limits the risk of further injury.

2. It decreases swelling. Swelling can prevent nutritious fluids from

reaching the injured area and increase pain by stretching the tissues. Too much swelling can press on and damage blood vessels and nerves.

Rest: Don't use the injured area any more than absolutely necessary. If a lower extremity is injured, walk as little as possible and use a crutch or cane. If an arm or hand is injured, use only your non-injured side. If your back is injured, don't lift, stoop or bend.

Ice: Injured tissues tend to leak fluid and blood. Ice applied in the correct manner lessens the leakage by constricting the blood vessels. Cover the ice pack with a cloth, or use cool water instead of ice. Apply the cold about ten to 15 minutes, then remove the cold for ten to 15 minutes. Repeat as needed. Applying ice directly or for too long can injure the tissue even more.

Compression: To limit swelling, wrap the injured area snugly (but not constricting) with a bandage, preferably elastic. Be sure you can place two fingers between the bandage and the skin. If you can't fit two fingers, the bandage is too tight. A little too much swelling can make a bandage that is too tight act like a tourniquet and cut off the circulation to a foot or hand.

 MOVEMENT DOESN'T INDICATE TYPE OF INJURY

The ability to move a body part or joint isn't an indication that the affected bone isn't broken. Even if a bone is broken, if the tendon is intact, you can move the joint unless the joint has been severely injured or is dislocated.

Elevation: Keep the injured area at heart level or above to decrease pain and limit swelling. If the injury is to a lower extremity, sit or lie down and elevate the foot. If it's an injured arm or hand, prop it on pillows or use a sling.

Splint: This is to immobilize the injured area to limit tissue damage and fracture movement. If you don't have a standard splint, use thick paper or a stick, or wrap the injury with thick clothes. To splint a finger, you can tape the injured digit to an adjacent, uninjured one.

HOW TO MAKE A SPLINT

- Use a splint stick or whatever stiff material you can find.

- Tie the splint in place with an elastic bandage, strips of cloth, a belt or whatever else you can find that works.

- Try to conform the material to the shape of the injury rather than trying to straighten a broken bone to conform to the splint.

- When splinting an injured joint, include the bones on both sides of the joint.

- When splinting an injured bone, include the joints on both sides of the bone.

SPINE INJURIES

The neck and back vertebrae (backbones) surround and protect the delicate spinal cord. A broken vertebra doesn't mean automatic paralysis, but if the fractured bone moves, even a little, it can injure the spinal cord and cause paralysis of the area below the injured level.

Spinal cord injuries of the neck usually result in paralysis of the arms, trunk and legs. They may also result in an inability to breathe and death. Injuries farther down the back may affect the trunk and legs, or the legs only. The more the fracture moves out of place, the more likely it may cause a serious cord injury and permanent paralysis.

How to Prevent Injury to the Spinal Cord

If someone has a possible head, neck or back injury, or even takes a bad fall, it is essential not to move the person until the spine can be checked out or stabilized—unless, of course, you're moving someone who's in imminent danger of, say, a fire, wild animal or falling rock.

Prevention Tip: In lieu of expert help and X-rays, you're going to make the best judgment call you can. If you cannot rule out an injury, always err on the side of not moving the person. Also, **you can never rule out a spine injury in someone who is unconscious or semiconscious** unless you saw the person pass out and know there was no injury to the head, neck or back. Otherwise, the spine must be protected until the person is fully conscious and can be trusted to make good judgment calls.

Tips to Rule Out a Broken Spine

1. **Press on each individual vertebra.** If any are tender, you must assume there could be a break. If the person is on his back, you'll have to reach under him, if you can, without moving him. The natural curves of the neck and lower back may make it easier to reach those areas. If you can't get to the back of the chest, press on each rib to see if the pressure causes referred pain to the spine.

2. **Check for feeling** with a safety pin, a stick or anything fairly sharp. Lightly scratch on both sides of each foot and each hand but not hard enough to risk further injury. If the person experiences numbness or a blunt feeling instead of sharp, you must assume the spine could be broken.

3. **Check muscle strength** by having the injured person move his toes first toward his head, then away from his head. Place your hand against the victim's foot to make sure he can move against a little resistance. Compare sides. Also have the person spread all his fingers and not let you close them when you press against them. If there is any significant weakness, assume the spine could be broken.

If any of the above findings are abnormal, you must protect the spine before you attempt any transfer of the person. Also, the person should be evacuated to a medical facility, whether it be by rescue team, helicopter, etc., if at all possible.

How to Protect the Spine

1. Surround the person's neck with firm material, such as a rolled-up blanket or sleeping bag, or even rolled-up newspapers. Of course if you have a commercial rigid cervical collar, use it. Make sure nothing is too tight that it could restrict blood flow or breathing. Move the head and neck as little as possible while doing this.

2. Find some stiff material that is longer than the person—some examples include a board, poles you've tied together or a door taken off its hinges. Place this make-do board next to the person.

3. It is very important that someone holds each side of the head to stabilize the neck at all times. The head should be positioned with the face looking straight ahead.

Treatment Tip: Until you're ready to move the person, a good way to hold the head steady is to kneel at the top of the victim's head. Place one of your knees on each side of the head and hold tight. This leaves your hands available for other work.

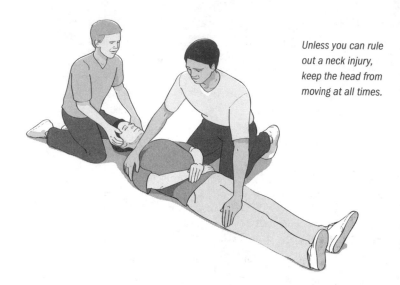

Unless you can rule out a neck injury, keep the head from moving at all times.

4. Move the person's head and shoulders so they're straight and facing the same way.

5. Straighten the legs.

6. Now try to slide the makeshift board underneath the person a bit. Then turn the person on her side, facing away from the board. Keep the spine stable by making sure that the victim's entire body turns at the same time. If there are two people to help, someone should hold the head and the other person hold at the hips. If there are three people, another should hold the shoulders. With four, someone could manage the feet. Everyone should move on the count of three. Keep the head, shoulders, hips and legs parallel all the time.

7. Place the board against the person's back and head.

8. With the board against the back and head, turn the person on her back again, using the board as support.

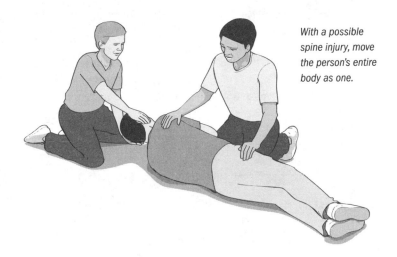

With a possible spine injury, move the person's entire body as one.

9. If the person is unconscious, consider keeping her on her side in case she vomits. Support one side of the board with pillows, cushions, cloths or whatever you have to keep the person on her side.

10. Regardless of position, stuff soft material in every space around and under the back and neck. Be sure to place material under the chin (but in a way that does not choke) so the person cannot move her head up and down or side to side. Consider stuffing something under the knees to flex them a little for comfort.

11. Wrap a blanket, or comparable material, around the person and board and firmly tie it down so she cannot move. Just be careful it's not so tight that it restricts blood flow or breathing.

RIB INJURIES

Rest, ice and over-the-counter pain medicines are the only treatment for most chest strains and bruises or rib fractures. Review the RICES method (see page 163) for proper icing techniques. Hold or brace the area of injury before a sneeze or cough.

Tight bandages that wrap around the chest may help the pain but don't help the healing process. They're not used anymore because they impede deep breathing and increase the risk for developing pneumonia.

There are complications that can develop with a rib cage injury including collapsed lung, tension pneumothorax, pneumonia and flail chest. The following sections detail these complications.

COLLAPSED LUNG

If a broken rib punctures the lung, air gets between the lung and the inside part of the chest wall (pneumothorax) and makes the lung smaller. The lung becomes less efficient in taking in air and oxygen. Bleeding (hemothorax) can decrease the lung size and make it less efficient. Either of these can cause pain and shortness of breath. However, if only one lung is affected, these complications are rarely life-threatening. There's nothing to do for this complication in the field unless the shortness of breath becomes pronounced.

Warning Signs of a Collapsed Lung After a Chest Injury

- shortness of breath

- decreased breath sounds on the side of the injury when listening to the chest with a stethoscope or ear

Treatment for Collapsed Lung

There is no treatment unless there is significant shortness of breath. A small pneumothorax or hemothorax is hard to find, and there's always the possibility of complications from the treatment, such as bleeding into the chest wall, infection or further damage to the lung.

If shortness of breath is severe, you can try to get the air or blood out by doing the following:

1. Clean the area with iodine, povidone-iodine, alcohol or soap and water.

2. Insert a long, hollow needle into the side of the chest (toward the back), just above one of the lower ribs.

Tension Pneumothorax

Sometimes the puncture wound in the lung acts like a one-way valve. When you breathe in, air goes through the leak and collects between the lung and chest wall. The air has no way to escape, so the more you breathe, the bigger the space gets until it starts pushing on the heart and aorta. This is a life-threatening emergency known as tension pneumothorax.

Warning Signs of Tension Pneumothorax

- progressive shortness of breath

- no breath sounds on the injured side of the chest when listening with a stethoscope or ear

- increasing pulse rate

- decreasing consciousness

- trachea (windpipe) that's deviated to the side away from the affected lung

- bulging neck veins

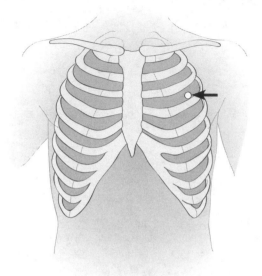

Where to insert the needle for emergency treatment of a tension pneumothorax.

Treatment of Tension Pneumothorax

1. Quickly clean the upper front of the chest on the side of the injury with iodine, povidone-iodine, alcohol or soap and water. If it's going to take more than a few seconds to find these supplies, skip this step.

2. Take a hollow needle—a long, large, 14-gauge angiocath (has a catheter over the needle) is ideal—and position it a couple of inches from the breastbone, just above the third rib (two ribs below the collarbone). Insert the needle slowly until you hear a hiss. Leave the needle in place if possible. If you are using an IV catheter such as an angiocath, take the needle out while leaving the catheter in place.

PNEUMONIA

Pneumonia may develop days, even weeks, after a chest injury.

Warning Signs of Pneumonia

- fever

- feeling bad

- increased pulse

- increasing shortness of breath, especially on exertion

Treatment

Antibiotics such as ciprofloxacin, erythromycin, clarithromycin or azithromycin can treat pneumonia. (See page 30 for more on how to get antibiotics.)

Plenty of rest and fluids is important. If the person is short of breath at rest, lethargic or not eating, it's important to try to get expert treatment such as oxygen and IV fluids.

FLAIL CHEST

If three or more ribs are broken on one side, and if each rib is broken in more than one place, the area between the breaks may not move in sync with the rest of the chest when you breathe in and out. This is called flail chest, and it severely limits the ability of the lung on that side to work properly.

Cushion the injured area and apply pressure or lie down with the injured side down. Immediate transfer to a medical facility is essential.

ACROMIOCLAVICULAR (AC) JOINT INJURIES

The acromioclavicular (AC) joint is located where ligaments attach the collarbone to the shoulder bone. Most people can find the AC joint as a bony protuberance on top of their shoulder. The injury is usually caused by a direct hit, which sprains the joint. It's also call an AC separation.

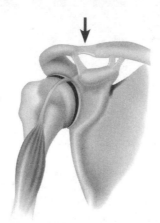

The AC joint can be found by following the collarbone to its end. In many people, the joint juts out a bit at the top of the shoulder.

How to Treat an AC Separation

- Use a sling for at least a week (see page 175). Depending on how badly the joint is sprained, you may need to keep your arm in the sling for up to six weeks. Without expert help, go with your own judgment but never less than a week.

- Follow the RICES method (see page 163).

CLAVICLE (COLLARBONE) INJURIES

A collarbone injury is usually the result of a direct blow or falling on an outstretched arm. The collarbone will be tender and may or may not be crooked.

How to Treat an Injured Collarbone

- A sling is the simplest treatment, and many doctors use it. Studies show that figure-of-eight splints work well for clavicle injuries, though they're harder to make in the field and more uncomfortable.

- Follow the RICES method (see page 163).

HOW TO MAKE A SLING

Cradle the forearm with a cloth or a wide belt and wrap the ends around your neck. Or wrap your shirttail around your forearm and safety pin the tail to a higher part of your shirt.

Keep the forearm cradled at around a 90-degree angle.

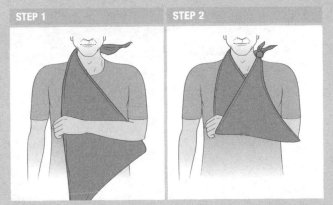

STEP 1 **STEP 2**

One way to make a sling is to fold a piece of cloth into a triangle shape. Wrap the wide part around your arm and tie the ends around your neck.

HUMERUS (UPPER ARM) INJURIES
The humerus includes the shoulder joint.

- Use a sling. If the upper arm or shoulder is broken, you'll need to wear the sling for at least six weeks.

- Follow the RICES method (see page 163).

**FIGURE-OF-EIGHT SPLINT FOR
A BROKEN COLLARBONE**

The purpose of the figure-of-eight splint is to keep the shoulders back in a constant extension. This position straightens out the collarbone so the fracture ends don't overlap. If you don't have a commercial splint, you can make one with an elastic bandage.

1. With the victim standing with his shoulders back and hands on his hips (like standing at attention), wrap the bandage around the uninjured shoulder to anchor the splint.

2. Now stretch the bandage from the top of that shoulder, across the back, to under the armpit of the injured side.

3. Wrap the bandage around the front of injured shoulder, over the top, and stretch it across the back and under the uninjured armpit.

4. Repeat until the whole bandage has been used. Pin or tape the end of the bandage in place.

ELBOW INJURIES

The immediate worry is trauma or swelling to the elbow that can injure adjacent arteries or nerves. Children are more susceptible to nerve and artery damage with an elbow injury, so pay even closer attention to them.

- Follow the RICES method (see page 163).

- It's more important than in most injuries to apply cold packs to limit swelling.

- Use a sling. If you can't feel a pulse in the wrist, try slowly and

TRACTION

Traction consists of grasping a hand or foot, or the end of a finger or toe, and pulling. Its purpose is to try to straighten a fracture or pull a dislocated bone far enough so it doesn't overlap and can move itself back into place. The key is gentle, but firm, consistent pulling. You may have to pull with increasing force for as much as a minute or two, but never jerk.

gently bending and straightening the elbow a little at a time and continue feeling for a pulse. If you can find a pulse, position the sling to keep the arm at that angle.

- If there's significant swelling, decreased feeling, decreased strength or no pulse, or the hand is turning dark and bluish, transfer to a medical facility is essential to try to prevent permanent damage.

FOREARM INJURIES

Your forearm contains two bones. The radius is the forearm bone on the thumb side. The ulna is the forearm bone on the little finger side.

- Follow the RICES method (see page 163).

- The splint (see page 165) should involve the forearm, wrist and hand, with the wrist cocked up slightly. At minimum, the splint should be placed under the forearm. If you have enough material, bend the elbow to about 90 degrees and make a U-shaped splint that goes across the palm, wrist and forearm, then wraps around the elbow and covers the upper arm, wrist and top of the hand.

- Use a sling (see page 175).

BONES AND JOINTS

- Even if the bones appear crooked, it's best to leave them alone if you expect to get expert help within a few days and as long as there's a good pulse in the wrist and the hand, and the fingers are not turning blue. Otherwise, you can try a little traction by grabbing the hand and pulling steadily.

WRIST, HAND AND FINGER INJURIES

A wrist injury can involve the small wrist bones, the end of one of the forearm bones or any combination of these.

- Follow the RICES method (see page 163).

- Splint the palm, the wrist and under the forearm (see page 165). If the splint will cooperate, cock the wrist upward slightly. You may need to wear the splint for up to six weeks.

- Use a sling (see page 175).

Splint an injured hand as you would the wrist, but make sure the splint comes down to the middle finger joints. Wrap the hand, preferably with an elastic bandage.

Splinting Fingers

To splint a finger, you can use:

- a ready-made splint

- a twig or stick

- a Popsicle stick

- a tongue depressor

- a "buddy splint"—tape the injured finger to an adjacent uninjured finger

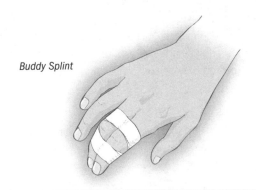

Buddy Splint

Treatment Tip: Some people try to pull or jerk on a jammed finger if a joint is painful or swollen. This does no good and may harm the joint. The only time to pull on the finger (apply traction) is if the finger is crooked or a joint is dislocated. With a dislocation, one bone is literally lying on top of the other, not just "jammed."

HIP AND THIGH INJURIES

Fractures of the hips and thighs are usually caused by falls or motor vehicle accidents.

A break in the middle of the thigh bone (femur) can cause major blood loss, even with minimal swelling. Immediate transfer to a medical facility is recommended.

If transfer is delayed or impossible for a mid-femur fracture, try the following:

1. Apply traction (see page 177) by pulling on the foot as it is in line with the rest of the leg (in a position as if walking). You have to pull hard (never jerk) because the thigh muscles are very strong and will react to the injury by contracting. Traction keeps the femur straight and pulls the thigh muscles around the break, causing them to compress and limit bleeding.

2. Unless you have a commercial traction splint for a hip or know how to make one, you can use a backboard, as described in the spinal injury section (see page 165), for splint and transfer.

KNEE INJURIES

The knee is a common area for fractures, sprains and torn cartilage and ligaments. Many times, it's difficult to know the specific type of injury that has occurred. Fortunately, first aid treatment is the same.

- Follow the RICES method (see page 163).

- If it hurts to bear weight, don't. Or do as little as possible by using a makeshift cane or crutches.

- If the knee feels unstable, splint it with a commercial brace or any firm material—sticks, rolled clothes, folded newspapers, etc. Then wrap it with an elastic bandage. The joint should be splinted straight, and the splint should include the lower thigh and upper part of the lower leg.

LOWER LEG INJURIES

Like the forearm, the lower leg contains two bones. The smaller, outside bone is the fibula. The inner, larger bone is the tibia. The tibia bears all the weight when you walk.

Tibia

If the tibia (inner, larger bone) is broken, splint the lower leg (see page 165) and don't bear weight or bear as little as possible, even with crutches or a cane.

- Follow the RICES method (see page 163).

Fibula

If this bone is broken and the tibia is not, you should still splint the lower leg (see page 165). But since the fibula is not the weight-bearing bone, it may be possible to walk with the help of crutches or a cane.

- Follow the RICES method (see page 163).

ANKLE INJURIES

This area includes the ankle bones and the ends of the fibula and tibia. Any or all of these bones can be broken, or any of the ligaments or tendons can be sprained.

- Follow the RICES method (page 163).

- Apply a brace or wrap the ankle with firm material followed by a bandage, preferably elastic.

- If firm material is not available, wrap the foot, ankle and lower part of the lower leg with an elastic bandage or some other cloth.

- High-top boots, laced tight, can substitute for a brace.

- Use a makeshift cane, as needed.

- Be very careful walking on an uneven surface or unfamiliar ground. It's very easy to retwist the ankle.

How to Apply a Figure-of-Eight Ankle Wrap

If you make sure the material you're using is rolled up, it will be easier to use.

1. Hold the loose end of the bandage against the side or top of the foot. Place it close to, but not including, the toes. Make one complete loop around the foot to secure the loose end in place. Wrap two more loops closer and closer to the ankle. Keep the bandage material taut while wrapping.

How to apply a figure-of-eight ankle wrap.

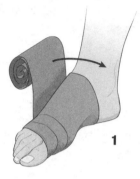 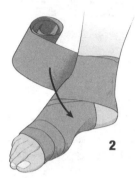

1

2

2. During the third loop, cross the material over the top of the foot and wrap it around the ankle.

3. Cross back over and wrap around the foot, then back around the ankle. The heel will stay bare.

4. Fasten the last of the material with the attached Velcro, clamps or your own safety pin or tape.

FOOT AND TOE INJURIES

A bone in the foot can break from an obvious injury, or the simple act of walking can cause a "stress" or "march" fracture. To prevent foot injuries, walk in a hard-sole shoe. Use a cane as needed. Never walk barefoot.

- Follow the RICES method (see page 163).

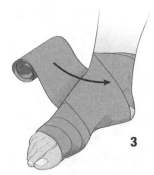 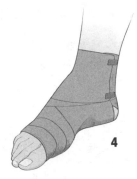

Toes

The great toe (biggest toe) bears most of the pressure when walking. An injury to it will potentially give you much more trouble than an injury to the other toes.

- If the toe is crooked, apply traction (page 177) to straighten it.

- Tape the injured toe to an adjacent uninjured one to create a buddy splint. If you have a dry cotton ball or some sort of cloth or gauze, place it between the toes before taping. This will cut down on skin damage from wetness and rubbing.

INDEX

traction, 95, 177, 179, 183
tweezers, 24

U
urinary tract infections, 32
urine concentration, 61
UV rays, for water disinfecting, 58–59

V
vaccines, 36–37, 112–113
vet wrap, 19
viruses, 32
vomiting, 62–65
    inducing, 160–161

W
wasp stings, 134
water, 48–65
    conserving, 52–53
    containers for, 51–52
    contaminants in, 53
    disinfecting, 29, 54–60
    filtering, 54
    microfiltration of, 59–60
West Nile virus, 143–145
worm infections, 33
wounds. *See also* skin wounds
    cleaning, 98–100
    closing, 102–106
    deciding on treatment for, 101–102
    gunshot, 116–121
    life-threatening, 95, 98
    unsticking dressing from, 18
wrist injuries, 178–179

Dedication

I dedicate this book to Pam, my wife. She's my constant support and the love of my life, and I thank God for her every day.

Acknowledgments

I could not have written this book without the generous assistance of my daughter Leigh Ann. From my blog to my videos to this book, she edits almost everything I do. My paramedic daughter, Beth, who has years of experience training military personnel, has also been indispensible (although she specifically asked me not to thank her). Thanks to my agent, Linda Konner, for sharing her wisdom and experience to make this project a reality. In addition, I thank all the folks at Living Ready—Patty, who guides me through the various media opportunities there, and Jackie, who has led me through the process of writing this book, all along providing helpful suggestions to improve the content.

About the Author

Dr. James Hubbard is a longtime family doctor who started out in small-town Mississippi, where his patients taught him generations-old home remedies. He has practiced in rural towns and big cities, in clinics and emergency rooms, and currently practices parttime at urgent care centers in Colorado.

In addition to his Doctor of Medicine degree, Dr. Hubbard has a master's in public health and is a member of the American Medical Association, American Academy of Family Physicians and American Academy of Occupational and Environmental Medicine.

Dr. Hubbard's other books include *The Survival Doctor's Guide to Wounds* and *The Survival Doctor's Guide to Burns*. He also writes for *American Profile* and *Living Ready* magazine and is a regular guest on survivalist Vincent Finelli's *USA Prepares* radio show. His website is TheSurvivalDoctor.com.

Other fine Living Ready books are available from your local bookstore and online suppliers. Visit our website at www.livingreadyonline.com. Living Ready® is a registered trademark of F+W Media.

17   16   15   14   5   4

ISBN 978-1-4403-3354-5

Distributed in Canada by Fraser Direct
100 Armstrong Avenue, Georgetown, Ontario, Canada L7G 5S4
Tel: (905) 877-4411

Distributed in the U.K. and Europe by F&W Media International, LTD
Brunel House, Forde Close, Newton Abbot, TQ12 4PU, UK
Tel: (+44) 1626 323200, Fax: (+44) 1626 323319
E-mail: enquiries@fwmedia.com

Distributed in Australia by Capricorn Link
P.O. Box 704, S. Windsor NSW, 2756 Australia
Tel: (02) 4560-1600
Fax: (02) 4577-5288
E-mail: books@capricornlink.com.au

Edited by Jacqueline Musser
Designed by Clare Finney
Production Coordinated by
Debbie Thomas

FIRST AID PACKING LIST FOR BUG OUT BAGS

Download the first aid packing list for bug out bags and hiking kits found in this book. The download is formatted in a convenient worksheet size that you can print and check off as you build or restock your first aid kit. Download the list for free at www.livingreadyonline.com/pocketfirstaid.

MORE BOOKS ON SURVIVAL AND PREPAREDNESS

Build The Perfect Bug Out Bag
By Creek Stewart

Prepper's Guide to Surviving Natural Disasters
by James D. Nowka

Build the Perfect Survival Kit, second edition
by John D. McCann

AVAILABLE ONLINE AND IN BOOKSTORES EVERYWHERE!

Join our mailing list at www.livingreadyonline.com.